"In *Sexpectations*, author Barb Winters gives all who love teenagers a great gift. She comes alongside responsible adults as they help the young people in their lives navigate the difficult world of relationships. Using a solid biblical foundation, she shares encouragement and solid structure to help us stay God-centered when tackling this hard subject. In this book, every reader is sure to find the hope and affirmation so needed in our world today."

—**Edie Melson,** award-winning author and Director of the Blue Ridge
Mountains Christian Writers Conference

"Barb Winters has done an incredible job addressing tough issues all families, churches, and youth groups face. As a therapist, school counselor, and mom of young adults, I'm grateful she is frank about the effects of a sexualized culture while also pointing to a better way in Christ. A must-read for all parents, youth leaders, and anyone needing to connect with today's youth."

—**Brenda Yoder,** Licensed Mental Health Counselor, School Counselor,
author of *Fledge: Launching Your Kids without Losing Your Mind*

"*Sexpectations* is a calming voice to parents in the midst of the chaos of trying to talk with older kids about sex. Barb candidly shares her own parenting journey to demonstrate that even when we do not do this perfectly, there can be hope for our kids. I appreciate how Barb goes beyond just 'what to say to kids' by including work we need to do as parents throughout this process. *Sexpectations* is an emotional rock for parents to stand on as they navigate these waters."

—**John Fort,** Director of Training at Be Broken Ministries

"Barb will help you understand the hookup culture and what has gone wrong with relationships, which is at the heart of pornography. But she won't leave you without a remedy. She gives hope for recovery and restoration. A big thank you goes to Barb Winters for addressing a topic not many Christian writers are brave enough to take on!"

—**Dena Yohe,** Cofounder of Hope for Hurting Parents and award-winning
author of *You Are Not Alone: Hope for Hurting Parents of Troubled Kids*

"Barb Winters offers a gift to parents and families learning to navigate a cultural minefield. This book is packed with relevant truths augmented with relatable illustrations. She identifies the pitfalls of unhealthy relationships, shares foundations for healthy ones, and provides principles to pursue recovery from wrong choices. *Sexpectations* meets contemporary needs by offering practical help. You'll find yourself referring to this valuable resource again and again."

—**Ava Pennington,** Bible Study Fellowship teacher and author of
Reflections on the Names of God

"As someone who has helped families dealing with porn addiction and sexual sin for twenty-four years, I can confidently say Barb does a great job addressing the issue in *Sexpectations*. This book is a powerful resource for any person or family trying to come to terms with habits for healthy relationships. More importantly, it will provide readers with real tools to help those they love to know how to heal and find sexual wholeness in Jesus Christ."

—**Dr. John Thorington,** author of *Pure Teens: Honoring God, Relationships, and Sex* and Owner/licensed therapist of Restoring Hearts Counseling

"Barb courageously takes her experience as a mom blindsided by porn and has written this tremendously valuable resource for others to help kids navigate today's hypersexualized culture. Nearly thirty years ago, my own addiction began at the age of ten when my older brother secretly brought pornography into the home. Had a book like *Sexpectations* been available then, I am certain the pain, shame, and isolation I experienced could have been avoided. Helping a child understand that pornography is not only outside God's design for sex but also creates unrealistic expectations will absolutely set them up for healthy relationships later."

—**Crystal Renaud Day,** MAPC, Founder of SheRecovery and author of
Dirty Girls Renewed

"When raising kids in an increasingly sexually broken world, it is no longer enough to pick up the wounded; we have to go on the offensive. Barb Winters has done an excellent job picking up the torch on behalf of caregivers everywhere by unflinchingly, thoroughly, and lovingly exposing the depth of the challenges before us—and the hope that can be found in proven, practical, Christ-centered solutions."

—**Rosie Makinney,** Founder of Fight For Love Ministries and author of *Fight For Love*

"*Sexpectations* is about so much more than sex. It provides a biblically sound roadmap to understand how culture has warped relationships and intimacy, and more importantly, how families can emerge strong and healthy, defying this distortion. Parenting in the digital age is one of the most challenging experiences any of us will ever have, and Barb shares her own stories with refreshing vulnerability. This book will supercharge your sense of purpose as a parent, giving you the courage and tools to connect more deeply with your kids and more resolutely stand against the toxicity of our culture."

—**Sarah Siegand,** Cofounder of Parents Who Fight

"Barb Winters presents a compelling, easy-to-understand guide for discussing the prevalent issues of sexting, pornography, and cultural immorality for today's youth. True change happens when we understand the mechanics behind an issue and can turn our eyes to God rather than lament the negative side effects of our toxic culture. As trusted adults in our children's lives, we need to arm ourselves with the right knowledge to rescue our kids from the influence of culture. Reading *Sexpectations* is an excellent step toward that goal."

—**Melanie Hempe,** BSN, Founder of ScreenStrong and author of *Can Your Teen Survive—and Thrive—Without a Smartphone?*

"I am excited Barb Winters has written *Sexpectations*. She is a fantastic resource for people looking for practical tips on how to talk with pre-teens and teens about healthy relationships amidst today's culture of pornography, social media, and hookups. I am confident her book will be a blessing to many."

—**Dr. John D. Foubert,** PhD, author of *Protecting Your Children from Internet Pornography* and board member of National Center on Sexual Exploitation (NCOSE)

sexpectations

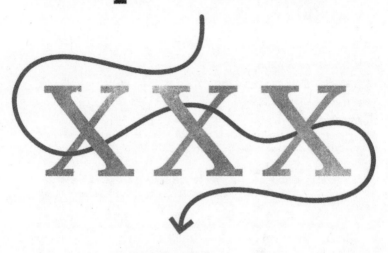

Helping the

Next Generation

Navigate Healthy

Relationships

Keep talking! Barb Winters ☺ #hopefulmom

BARB WINTERS

LEAFWOOD
P U B L I S H E R S
an imprint of Abilene Christian University Press

SEXPECTATIONS

Helping the Next Generation Navigate Healthy Relationships

L E A F W O O D
P U B L I S H E R S
an imprint of Abilene Christian University Press

Published in association with The Blythe Daniel Agency, Inc., PO Box 64197, Colorado Springs, CO 80962.

LIBRARY OF CONGRESS CATALOGING-IN-PUBLICATION DATA
Names: Winters, Barb, author.
Title: Sexpectations : helping the next generation navigate healthy relationships / by Barb Winters.
Description: Abilene, Texas : Leafwood Publishers, 2023.
Identifiers: LCCN 2022049791 | ISBN 9781684262120 | ISBN 9781684268832 (ebook)
Subjects: LCSH: Sexual ethics—Religious aspects—Christianity. | Christian ethics. | Sexual behavior.
Classification: LCC HQ32 .W537 2023 | DDC 176/.4—dc23/eng/20230309
LC record available at https://lccn.loc.gov/2022049791

Cover design by Thinkpen Design, LLC | Interior text design by Sandy Armstrong, Strong Design

Leafwood Publishers is an imprint of Abilene Christian University Press
ACU Box 29138, Abilene, Texas 79699

1-877-816-4455 | www.leafwoodpublishers.com

23 24 25 26 27 28 29 / 7 6 5 4 3 2 1

To all the parents, grandparents, and caregivers navigating this world of hookups, pornography, and all things online with their children, especially those who've been surprised by a child's unhealthy choices. You are not alone. I see you.

Contents

the deterioration
of relationships

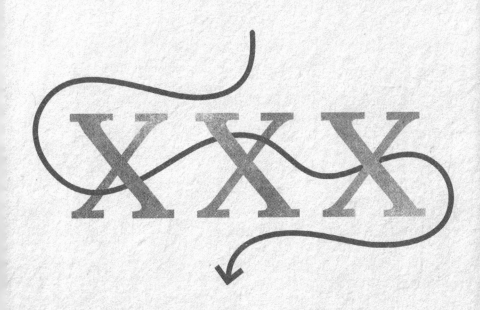

As Long as You're Happy

*The world looks for happiness through self-assertion. The
Christian knows that joy is found in self-abandonment.
"If a man will let himself be lost for My sake," Jesus
said, "he will find his true self."* —Elisabeth Elliot[1]

After a church service, Michelle, a friend nearing retirement, stopped me to chat.

"I haven't seen Sue in a while. How's she doing?" she asked about our mutual friend.

"One of Sue's sons moved in with his girlfriend."

"Oh, really?" Michelle's mouth dropped.

I wasn't sure if she was surprised by the situation itself or because she hadn't already heard this news. Ignoring Michelle's reaction, I shared that Sue was heartbroken and still processing her son's new living arrangements.

Her reply? "Well, as long as he's happy. That's all that matters."

I blinked. What could I say? It wasn't the time or place to argue biblical principles. Besides, she was only repeating a common comeback. I nodded politely and moved the conversation to a different topic.

We Hold These Truths

Whether the statement is meant as consolation or the sender truly believes it, I hear *as long as you're happy* or some form of this phrase frequently, both inside and outside church walls. I understand this sentiment from someone who doesn't subscribe to God's Word, but this opinion within the Christian community is puzzling.

How have we strayed so far from biblical principles? Even the older generation isn't sad when hearing someone lives outside God's teaching. How did we get to the point that even within church settings we send the message that happiness trumps godliness? And how does this affect the future of the church? More importantly, how does it affect our children's future?

> How did we get to the point that even within church settings we send the message that happiness trumps godliness?

Being happy isn't bad. After all, the United States Declaration of Independence says we are all created equal and possess rights our Creator gifted to us, including the right to pursue happiness. From the beginning of the country, Americans have been inspired and encouraged to pursue happiness.

We see it in the media. In the 2006 movie *The Pursuit of Happyness*, based on a true story, the main character is a single dad. He invests his money in a product that doesn't sell well and finds himself residing on the streets with his son while trying to earn a living. At first, he's unsuccessful, but he eventually meets a businessman who, through a series of events coupled with hard work, propels him into a lucrative career. The movie promotes the idea that anyone can be happy regardless of lineage, upbringing, or status.

But does the constitutional right to pursue happiness equate to seeking it as an end goal? And does the means for obtaining it make a difference?

We can conclude, based on their writings, that our forefathers didn't intend for us to seek self-gratification with no thought of others. Rather, they wanted us to know that our freedoms extend beyond dwelling in a land with no king—we have the freedom to choose a lifestyle that produces our best selves. Our lives don't need to be directed by a monarchy. Instead, we can use our God-given intellect to make personal decisions.

Certainly, God wants us to be happy—to enjoy life. But, as we will explore later, genuine joy comes from him, not from seeking a life of pleasure.

As Long as . . .

The portion of the statement that sends it askew is the qualifier *as long as*. Where are the boundaries in this phrase? Is it okay to eat an entire chocolate cake *as long as I'm happy*? Can I drink until I can't stand up *as long as I'm happy*? What if I quit my job and can't pay my bills *as long as I'm happy*?

What if the statement is turned against me and becomes *as long as they're happy*? Is it okay for my date to flirt with another person in the middle of our outing *as long as he's happy*? Is it okay for a parent to leave a child home alone all night *as long as the parent is happy*? Can we treat other humans as objects *as long as we're happy*? Is it acceptable to murder your companion *as long as you're happy*? Where is the line in this type of reasoning? Are there limitations?

The *as long as you're happy* people may now be thinking, "Well, that's taking it a little far." But isn't that how society inched its way to this disposition to begin with? By pushing the line just a little, and then a little more? We've been pushing that line for so long, we don't know where the plumb line is anymore. We don't know where we started or how to get back.

Happiness as an End Goal

What's wrong with being happy? Nothing. But happiness is fleeting. It's based on emotions and circumstances, whereas joy comes from the Lord and is an internal state of being. Pursuing happiness purely for happiness's sake doesn't allow for the tension created by God's refining process when we seek him. It opposes the pursuit of God first and gaining joy as a natural outcome. His Word states, "Those who look to him for help will be radiant with joy; no shadow of shame will darken their faces" (Ps. 34:5 NLT).

Happiness is not universally definable or measurable. Goals should be specific and measurable. Since happiness is subjective, how will we know if we've achieved it? And what if we finally "arrive" at that feeling we've been chasing, and it's yanked away the next moment by something out of our control? We become frustrated and angry.

A focus on happiness minimizes a sense of personal responsibility for poor choices or wrong decisions. It curtails the desire to stick it out and work through the rough times. If a pleasure seeker isn't happy in a relationship, she moves on. A church friend might even comfort her with the statement, "God must have someone out there who's better for you."

> A focus on happiness minimizes a sense of personal responsibility for poor choices or wrong decisions.

This self-gratifying attitude is not fulfilling. While one may experience temporary bliss, it's short-lived and lacks satisfaction and true peace. It doesn't deliver what is promised.

An *as long as you're happy* mentality within the church supports these false messages:

- **Happiness is more important than being content with God's plans.** We've elevated the pursuit of happiness above God's Word and seeking his will for our lives. If we don't sense abundant glee, we assume we aren't in the right place at the right time. We haven't learned how to patiently listen and wait for his peace to fill us.
- **If we aren't experiencing happiness, we aren't following God.** We've been conditioned to believe the litmus test for whether we're in God's will is how we feel. But sometimes God allows discomfort to expose insecurities or sinful behaviors, ours or someone else's.
- **To find our calling, we should ask, "How can I be happy?"** Rather than asking this question, maybe we should ask, "How can I pursue God and his will for my life?" He created us and will point us toward goals generating deep-felt joy. "Take delight in the LORD, and he will give you the desires of your heart" (Ps. 37:4).

This underlying "chase what brings you pleasure" state of mind has trickled down to millennials and Gen Zers. Many are bold, outspoken, and stand up for themselves—all great qualities. At the same time, constant accessibility to computers and smartphones, coupled with teachings from their predecessors, conditions them to seek whatever brings them immediate bliss. The result is that today's children and young adults face heavy loads of anxiety, worry, and depression.[2] Many are lost, insecure, and wishing for something better.

The younger generations are growing up in a world of pornographic images as sex teachers and hookups as goals, with peers and influencers shaping their well-being. Their culture celebrates individuality and, at times, emotionless relationships, if you can call them that. Thankfully, parents are recognizing that their children need help.

Let's explore this *as long as you're happy* world they are growing up in, starting with hookup culture.

What Is Hookup Culture?

An increasing number of preteens, teens, college students, and even older singles have an indifferent attitude toward casual sex. It's becoming an accepted, even celebrated, norm.[3]

Donna Freitas, a professor and researcher, lists three criteria for a hookup in her article, "A Good Samaritan Response to Hookup Culture." A hookup is brief, from five minutes to all night; it includes some type of sexual intimacy, anything from just kissing to intercourse; and, most importantly, it takes place with the assumption that there will be no emotional, or otherwise, attachment. When the encounter is over, each person walks away with no expectations. The iffy criterion is alcohol. College students who take part in hookups are known to drink before and during a hookup party.[4]

In the same article, Freitas distinguishes a hookup from hookup culture. Hookup culture sells the idea that it's normal to have an attitude of ambivalence toward sex and one's partner. The notion that college students, in general, are hooking up and are okay with it is promoted and encouraged within hookup culture.

In order to appear normal, students act as if they approve of hookup culture. They are purposefully vague in their description of a rendezvous, keeping the details mysterious or ambiguous. Whether they only kissed for a few minutes or spent the night together, both women and men can hide behind the word *hookup*. They can brag of participating in hookup culture without exposing themselves as either prudish or promiscuous, thus protecting their reputation and keeping up appearances at the same time.

Individuals engage in these meetups for several reasons. We may assume attraction is the main purpose, but it's actually a desire to fit in, which is a type of peer pressure. Because the culture says hooking up is common, individuals feel obligated to participate just to prove themselves as normal.[5] But humans are *not* naturally indifferent. Therefore, participants walk away unfulfilled. Students are left feeling empty or desiring an attachment but are reluctant to listen to their inner promptings.

Widespread Acceptance

At first glance, hookup culture seems primarily confined to college campuses. However, if we pay closer attention to our surroundings, we notice mainstream media, including sponsored ads and posts on social media and shows on streaming apps like Netflix, reference hookups frequently. These sexual encounters are purely for self-pleasure and come with no intended commitment. While this behavior has a greater reputation within student life, it's also promoted by corporations and individuals via media and advertisements as standard conduct for all singles, regardless of age or lifestyle.

My family and I watched a few episodes of *New Girl*, a television series that first aired in 2011. The show features three men and a woman who share an apartment. From the outset, it's apparent that the primary aim of each character is to hook up with someone, anyone. They even talk about "hooking up" multiple times. Within the first few episodes, the three men living with Jess, the female roommate, encourage her to find a partner for rebound sex after a breakup.[6] On a separate occasion, one of the guys attends a wedding specifically to locate a hookup buddy.[7] The characters believe casual sex will solve their problems. Lonely? Hook up. Hurt? Hook up. Mad? Hook up. Then all will be right in the world. Until it isn't. Because, inevitably, whatever problem existed to begin with remains after the sex is over.

Since the series won the Critics' Choice Television Award for Most Exciting New Series in its first season and was still a favorite on Netflix at the time of this book's publication, it's safe to assume people watch and are influenced by its messages.[8]

Evolution of Hookup Culture
Hookup culture did not originate with Netflix, though.

According to researcher Justin Garcia, hookups became more frequent in the 1920s because people began purchasing cars; therefore, youth were able to leave their homes to date. Their parents weren't close in proximity, so they felt freer to explore their sexuality.[9] This is also the time period when courting morphed to dating as speakeasies, bars, and movie theaters became common places where young men and women could socialize.[10]

The sexual revolution during the 1960s brought the concept that sex doesn't need to be tied to marriage or even a monogamous relationship. It is interesting to note that the pill became available in 1960. This newfound freedom for women meant they didn't need to associate sex with procreation. Women felt empowered and began to express their desire for sexual pleasure. Although some groups blamed oral contraceptives for changes in the United States, the article "The Pill and the Sexual Revolution" on *PBS* explains that historians now think the pill did not actually cause the sexual revolution. Instead, these forces worked together to foster the emerging hookup culture.[11]

The popularity of television, movies, music, and advertising contributed to the influence of the media on the culture. According to Lisa Wade, author of *American Hookup: The New Culture of Sex on Campus*, movies like *Animal House* portrayed college as more than a place to get an academic degree or even find a spouse.[12] College was the place to sow your oats, have fun, and party hard. And this idea stuck.

My Experience in the 1980s

When I began researching hookup culture, I assumed I knew nothing about it. I grew up in the 1980s and figured hooking up was a newer phenomenon. I asked others about their experiences and had an enlightening conversation with a friend in her early thirties. She was sexually active in high school and became a mom at the age of sixteen. The baby's father left, and for a few years after her daughter was born, she continued to seek fulfillment through one-night stands.

"On the weekends, I dressed up in my cutest clothes and went to parties. We stood around a bonfire and glanced about, hoping to catch someone's eye. No one wanted to go home by themselves at the end of the night."

When she mentioned a bonfire, I thought, *Wait a minute. I know this scene. I've lived this scene.* Suddenly, I was sixteen again and standing around a bonfire next to a keg, clinging to my red Solo cup filled with beer. I feared being left alone and wished the guy I had a crush on would ask me to "go with him," the term used for dating.

In high school, my friends and I broke onto the back nine of the golf course at the local country club to hang out and drink. If we found someone old enough to purchase alcohol for us, we drank wine coolers—the cheapest brand available, of course. Otherwise, we were stuck drinking whatever alcoholic beverage someone offered us.

Occasionally, we drove to a classmate's home in the country, lit a bonfire, and drank around the keg until curfew. The highest form of acceptance, at least in my eyes, was either arriving with a guy or leaving with one. When I rode with a girlfriend, I hoped she wouldn't abandon me or that my latest infatuation would strike up a conversation, proving he was attracted to me.

At one such party, the big bash kicking off the high school football season, I drank so much I could barely stand. My ride had an earlier curfew than me. Thinking it was better to wait that extra hour to sober up before greeting my parents at the front door, I accepted a new guy friend's offer to take me home. Along the way, we stopped at his house. I only remember two things about this detour: I knocked something off a shelf in his bathroom while trying to be as quiet as possible, and it began to snow on the way to my house. The rest of the night is a blur.

I saw him the next day in English class. I had no clue what, if anything, to say to this guy who had driven me home in his fancy car. Had we kissed? Had we gone further than kissing? Did he consider me his girlfriend? In the end, I said nothing. And neither did he.

That night scared me enough to take note of my drinking limitations but didn't stop me from pursuing *the* guy, whoever he might be, who would make me the happiest girl on earth. The party hopping continued, and I had more encounters I'm not proud of.

Through the discussion with my younger friend, I learned that even I grew up in a hookup culture. While I may have been hoping for a long-term relationship, the guys weren't. However, the attitude of the latest generation toward hookups is a ramped-up version, one that exploded with the introduction of smartphones in the first decade of the 2000s.

Now everyone has access to whatever they want whenever they want it, regardless of whether the information is true or false. And there is plenty of false information regarding what makes someone happy and how to find pleasure in a relationship, including the pornography available at our fingertips.

The Online Pornographic World

Pornography has exacerbated the idea that hooking up is normal, natural, and a perfectly acceptable means to satisfaction. What many parents don't understand is that today's pornography is readily available, more graphic and violent than ever, and out to capture the minds of our children. It's nothing like the *Playboy* of yesteryear. While my generation had to plan ahead to watch an inappropriate video, today's children stumble onto an image or video clip while innocently scrolling. Young kids who are too young to run a vacuum or cook on the stove search for a word they don't know and become exposed to a whole new world. Advertisements appear on their sidebar as they complete a homework assignment. Curiosity gets the better of them, and they click. One click is all it takes. Just like you and I get lost on Facebook, Instagram, or YouTube, clicking one video after another, they are off and running, accessing free pornography easily.

> Pornography has exacerbated the idea that hooking up is normal, natural, and a perfectly acceptable means to satisfaction.

But children don't just search for it on their own or stumble onto it accidentally. Sometimes, their friends show them. Kids are eager to share their newfound knowledge and freely stick their devices with the offensive material under the innocent eyes of their friends or even acquaintances. I've heard stories from mom friends stating that their six-year-old or seven-year-old was shown photos or videos during sports practices, playdates, or during school. One mom told me that a nine-year-old girl showed her ten-year-old son pornography while both parents were in the same room. Sometimes our young children report these incidents to us because they are shocked by what they see or understand the dangers. But many times, especially if no one has talked with them about pornography, they don't say anything.

Pornography was in our home for years without my knowledge. The day I learned that my fourteen-year-old son watched porn, I was blindsided. I felt a gag reflex at the back of my throat when I heard him say, "I was watching porn." *What?! How could that be?* I thought I had misheard or that I was living someone else's life. We taught our children biblical principles and the difference between right and wrong. We homeschooled them and took them to church. My husband was a pastor. I thought all those components equated to raising children who knew when to say "no" to worldly pleasures. But I was wrong.

My son was watching pornography when a bogus warning popped up on his screen that threatened him to pay money or the person on the other end would call the police. He was petrified at the thought of being arrested and, out of fear, came to his dad and me in a panic. That day changed my life. I can still visualize my son standing in our yard and revealing this secretive information to us. My eyes were opened to an underground world I didn't know or understand. The shock, pain, hurt, anger, shame, and feeling of loneliness changed the trajectory of my life.

But porn isn't the only negative influence smartphones brought with them. Social media affects what we think of ourselves and how we interact with others. These virtual communities have upped the comparison game and set our emotions on edge. One moment we are riding a high created by extra likes and flattering comments, and the next we are facedown in our pillow reeling from one semi-negative comment said by someone we've never met. And whatever emotional roller coaster we are riding, our children are on one going four times as fast with steeper hills and more curves, twists, and turns.

> Whatever emotional roller coaster we are riding, our children are on one going four times as fast with steeper hills and more curves, twists, and turns.

Devices granting access to anyone at any time ushered in a new way of introducing yourself to a potential partner. Whether searching for a long-term relationship or a quick fix to a sexual need, sending a nude, or sexting, is now equivalent to saying hello. Per Camille Mori, Jessica E. Cooke, and others in "The Prevalence of Sexting Behaviors among Emerging Adults: A Meta-Analysis," not only is consensual sexting an emerging behavior, but so is nonconsensual sexting.[13]

I was at a small group with some church friends and was explaining how middle schoolers send nudes on a regular basis when one of the ladies shared her experience. "Before my husband and I got married a few years ago, I was on several Christian single dating sites. Men sent me unsolicited photos of their penises all the time." This is a grown woman with adult children who was receiving photos of what used to be private parts.

Another friend, a single lady in her thirties, chimed in. "Yep. I've been on those sites. Happened to me, too."

All I could think was, *Ew. Who wants to see that?*

The 2020 pandemic and lockdown intensified this hookup culture and pornographic atmosphere. What already existed worsened. With children and adults alike spending an unprecedented amount of time staring at screens all day, it was the perfect storm for the pornography industry and predators to capture the attention of more consumers. Thankfully, the pandemic also brought attention to what most hadn't known or had ignored—pornography and groomers for human trafficking are in our neighborhoods. And we began discussing it.

I work part-time with a nonprofit and go to local schools to talk with middle schoolers and high schoolers about making healthy choices. Recently, I was talking with eighth graders about avoiding risky behaviors, and I mentioned the dangers of sending and receiving nudes. After class, one of the girls came up to me. "Some old man sent me a pic of his private stuff. It was gross, so I reposted it for my friends to see." She laughed. She didn't find it odd, nor did she understand that even two decades ago, this type of behavior would be shocking and shunned.

She and her classmates, as well as most middle schoolers, are under the impression that these actions are ordinary and acceptable. If another student, especially one a preteen or teen is attracted to, asks for a nude, she sends it. Even those who hesitate for moral reasons sometimes give in because of peer pressure. While teaching, I'm quick to point out that sending and receiving nudes at their age is possession of and distribution of child sexual abuse material (also known as child pornography).[14] It also opens doors to sexual exploitation, sex trafficking, sextortion, and revenge porn.

While my adult friend could dismiss an unsolicited nude as obnoxious and vulgar, an eighth grader can't use the same logic to distinguish right from wrong, especially since she has no other frame of reference. This is a major problem with hookup culture, a porn-saturated world, and noses in screens all day. Many who belong to younger generations can't discern healthy from unhealthy, positive from negative, godly from ungodly because they don't have files stored in their brains to analyze scenarios against. And as they continue to make poor choices, their physical brains are altered.

Brain Development
I opened my car door, slipped into the seat, fastened my seatbelt, and started the ignition. I pulled out of the driveway and drove

two miles. My car turned left, and suddenly, I was sitting in the church parking lot. That's when I realized I couldn't remember how I got there.

Has this happened to you? You've repeated a task for so long and so often, you no longer need to think through the steps. They're automatic. And, at times, you wonder how you accomplished the deed that has become so mindless it no longer requires concentration. These mechanical practices, born from repetitive behavior, are a marvel.

The area of brain science is growing and receiving a lot of attention. What we've learned is our brains form grooves, or neurological pathways, based on our decisions. Each time we make the same choice, the groove deepens. The deeper the groove, the more difficult it is to modify. These grooves are helpful when the involuntary habit we've formed is positive, like learning the steps to driving a car. But not all routine responses are constructive.

Our children's brains are particularly vulnerable because they are still developing. A brain is not fully mature until the midtwenties. Until then, the pleasure-seeking part, the amygdala, is in battle with the logical part, the prefrontal cortex. The prefrontal cortex, the portion of the brain responsible for planning ahead and understanding cause and effect, is the last to develop. Therefore, teens depend on their amygdala and are susceptible to instinctual decisions that lead to risky behaviors.

The portion we adhere to affects future outcomes. If a decision is based on the intelligent, logical, sensible section of the brain, the same choice becomes easier in the future. However, if we cave into the pleasure-seeking, irrational part and make choices solely based on instant gratification, those same choices become easier and easier until they're automatic.

Furthermore, the dopamine hit our brain receives after pleasurable behaviors produces a desire for more of those rewarding deeds. And when those same actions no longer satisfy our cravings, we want more and more. This is why we see dangerous challenges on TikTok or Instagram go viral. Our brain craves the dopamine hit caused by more likes, shares, and comments. The rational portion of our brain may be saying, *This is too dangerous. It's not worth the time and effort.* But we don't listen because we are gliding down those deep grooves created by memories of the neurochemical reward boost our body receives when we experience unending scrolling, likes, shares, etc.

As certain behaviors continue, the status quo is less satisfying. Therefore, cravings may intensify. What could have quenched a desire one day leaves the brain seeking more the next. This explains why a one-night stand is less satisfying than it used to be and why porn users may require more usage at more violent levels to feel gratified.

The good news is that the brain is neuroplastic, which means it's pliable. The brain can form new pathways and heal itself, even as an adult. Still, a teen's brain is more impressionable and prone to forming long-term addictions because the prefrontal cortex is developing. The pathways formed through habitual decisions as a teen are not as easy to overcome.

In the Bible, we find this thought in the middle of the "love chapter": "When I was a child, I talked like a child, I thought like a child, I reasoned like a child. When I became a man, I put the ways of childhood behind me" (1 Cor. 13:11). We will explore the full passage later in the book, but I find it fascinating that while talking about love and exploring its many facets, God inserts information about our intellect. Scripture confirms that our mental ability to think logically and make rational decisions should improve as we grow up. But if that reasoning is stifled or stunted based on faulty information or lack of self-control, the brain will not function properly as an adult.

We want to turn the flawed reasoning around in our minds and in those of our children. This hookup culture, this society that says watching pornography is acceptable and having more friends on social media is our objective, seen through an *as long as you're happy* lens, is destroying relationships.

If we persist in holding up the pursuit of happiness and continue to tout the *as long as you're happy* mentality as the end-all fix to everything wrong, relationships will continue to deteriorate, including relationships with friends, coworkers, spouses, children, and God.

> If we persist in holding up the pursuit of happiness and continue to tout the *as long as you're happy* mentality as the end-all fix to everything wrong, relationships will continue to deteriorate.

Our approach needs adjusted. Our perspective needs shifted.

Maybe we're setting our sights too low. We are shortchanging ourselves by desiring mere happiness. We're looking to purchase a three-bedroom home in a cute neighborhood when God wants to hand us a mansion on the beach. Let's change our target and aspire to experience the deeper, richer satisfaction and contentment that accompanies the joy found only in God. This joy is fulfilling and long-lasting. Rather than aiming for a short-lived emotion, our goals should revolve around pursuing God and his righteousness. When we lean into him, we have joy and experience happiness.

Consequences of Unhealthy Choices

Then Jesus declared, "I am the bread of life. Whoever comes to me will never go hungry, and whoever believes in me will never be thirsty." (John 6:35)

I was sitting on my lanai when my phone rang. A mom I recently met was on the other end. "My daughter needs to have a procedure on her female parts."

"I'm sorry to hear that."

"I'm worried the STD [sexually transmitted disease] she caught in college will affect her ability to have children. She's been having problems for a couple of years. I hope this latest diagnosis and upcoming treatment fixes the issue."

I knew a little of the daughter's history because her mother and I had spoken about her previous sexual activities before. This

mom was pretty sure her daughter had slept with multiple partners during the four years she attended the nearby university. Her
daughter had talked with her about the emotional trauma a few
of those encounters caused. She'd even wondered if one instance
could've been considered rape.

I didn't ask the mom which disease her daughter had, but I
knew, based on training for my job, that gonorrhea and chlamydia,
two of the most common STDs, cause PID (pelvic inflammatory
disease). If untreated, PID leads to ectopic pregnancies or infer-
tility. With these two in particular, but with others also, a woman
in her reproductive years may not know she's contracted an STD
because they can be asymptomatic. When she's ready to conceive
and can't, a trip to the doctor uncovers the truth. The STD damaged her organs, and she isn't able to get pregnant. While the
disease may be curable, the damage is irreversible.

"Thanks for calling me. I'll be praying for you and your daughter. Please keep me posted on how she's doing and the outcome of
the procedure." I hung up the phone.

I'm sure this young lady had no idea the decisions she made in
college would one day affect her ability to bear children. Like most
teens, she probably didn't stop to ponder how one choice would
affect her the next day, much less years down the road. More than
likely, she only saw the potential benefits to her behavior.

What are the advantages, real or perceived, to hooking up?
Why would adolescents, young adults, or even older adults choose
to take part in this *casual sex is where it's at* environment? What
are they seeking? And are they finding it? Is this lifestyle living up
to its reputation?

Driving Forces

In the first chapter, we looked at the pursuit of happiness as an underlying reason to chase sexual encounters. Admittedly, there's a moment of fulfillment at the culmination of the sex act as our bodies are flooded with hormones. For some, the quest adds to the pleasure. But are these moments worth the hype, especially in the long run?

Sleeping around is like rolling the dice with our physical and emotional well-being, but that's not the message teens receive from their peers and the media. Yes, they've heard the possible physical consequences. Most sat through lectures on STDs and potential pregnancies, but they don't believe it will happen to them, think the evidence is inaccurate, or don't care. Additionally, the information they hear in school may contradict what they witness at home. If parents, caregivers, and grandparents aren't modeling healthy interactions, the chances a child will understand and experience healthy relationships drops.

While working with parents of children who've been exposed to pornography, I've interacted with a few who think watching porn as an adult is okay. While I agree that the ramifications aren't as severe if this behavior begins after the brain has matured, pornography doesn't illustrate healthy sexual activity. Our children, regardless of age, aren't automatically immune to negative influences. Young adults can't magically distinguish between right and wrong, good and bad, once they turn eighteen. Adolescents who grow up in homes where adults watched pornography are more likely to think the acts they're viewing in pornographic videos are normal. They may not understand they could form emotional, physical, and chemical attachments to the images on the screen.

One-night stands and the anonymity of watching pornography give the illusion of freedom. As society swings toward a me-centered posture, as depicted by the selfish undertones in hookup culture and the porn industry, attitudes are shifting. The perception, backed by messages in the media, is that life is found in fun, that fun is found in sex, and that sex is better without emotional attachment.

The perception of satisfaction, the pursuit of happiness, and the desire to be free—free to make one's own choices and free from the control of others—are driving forces to seeking sexual gratification while staying emotionally disconnected. But the answer isn't to eliminate emotional attachment to people.

Many have witnessed unhealthy relationships in their homes or desire to stay unattached in order to pursue personal goals. Whatever the reason, the youngest generation, like generations before them, doesn't want to be confined by their parents' or grandparents' values, which, as discussed in Chapter One, are moving further away from biblical principles.

I'm not saying parents are uncaring or clueless or that older generations aren't progressing in certain areas. We're a work in progress.

We're learning the importance of taking care of ourselves. Self-care, soul care, and living in reality, as opposed to pretending everything is fine, is healthy. Identifying emotions and pinpointing their origin, while comparing the results of this analysis to Scripture and saturating the findings in prayer, is the start to a fulfilling and purposeful life.

Is this type of self-evaluation, this type of self-care, being passed down to the next generation? Are they being taught who God is by their elders? Do they read his Word and have a relationship with him? Do they lean on God when they have issues? Have they learned how to work through difficult circumstances based on Scripture?

Some have. Some haven't. Even those of us who have a relationship with Christ and logically understand why we need to follow God's statutes still live in and are influenced by the culture around us. We need to wrestle with our attitudes, our way of thinking, and how God's Word fits with the world we dwell in. As the standards of society change, we can look at our thoughts, opinions, and postures. Are we helping or hindering? Are we moving closer to God and allowing him to refine us, or are we buying what the world is selling? Are we modeling how to do life well, how to have healthy relationships? If not, how can we begin?

Let's start by looking at a recipe that may lead to unhealthy relationships:

self-doubt + no relationship with Christ + everyone's doing it = a perpetual cycle of unhealthy relationships

I want to break this down and explore each component.

Self-Doubt

I sat down at the dinner table, looked around, and said to my son, "You forgot the salad tongs again. Please grab them from the drawer. The list of items to set the table is on the refrigerator. It's been on the refrigerator for a year. There are only six items on the list. How can you forget something every single night?"

I'm not sure how often I spoke some version of these words when my children were young—at least twice a week for a couple of years. We had three boys. They took turns setting the table. Almost every night, they forgot the forks or the salad dressings or the glasses. It drove me crazy. I couldn't understand why reading a list of six items and verifying everything was on the table was so difficult for a ten-year-old.

We adopted our daughter when she was five and a half. She observed her brothers set the table for two weeks when she decided to give it a try. She got it right the first time. Every single object was on the table in its proper place. This is all the more impressive because she couldn't speak or read English. She learned by watching. My husband jokingly said, "Wow. You boys have been snowing us all these years. Your sister just showed you up. If she can do it, you can do it."

Reasoning skills, life experience, and personality types factor into a person's desire to excel and pay attention to detail.[1] Our daughter was eager to please her new parents by showing how much she could accomplish, while our boys didn't care about performing the task to my liking. But I often wonder if things would have been different if I could travel back in time and encourage my children differently. Could we have had more pleasant experiences at suppertime? Would my boys have felt more confident in their skills and abilities?

I've heard it takes somewhere between three and six positive comments to combat one negative comment, but practicing that suggestion requires planning. I wasn't the type to look at my ten-year-old and say, "Wow. You did a great job putting the salad on the table. I love how you placed the forks on top of the napkins. And your selection of salad dressings is perfect. But I don't see any salad tongs. Can you grab those out of the drawer before you sit down? And next time, check the list before assuming you're finished setting the table." That seems, well, extra. By suppertime, I was tired.

Unfortunately, I didn't consider how my blunt words affected my children's thoughts about themselves. I love to encourage people, but I'm also businesslike. I'm the First Impressions director at our church and have caught myself on a Sunday morning asking questions about why tables have been moved or why the trash is overflowing before saying hello to anyone. In my zeal to spruce up the church for guests, I've unintentionally hurt volunteers or left them believing they haven't met my standards, which is a form of rejection. Yes, I see the irony.

This is not to say I've never complimented my church friends or my children. As a homeschool mom, I did my best to bolster their self-worth and foster their character. But I'm not sure I ever hit the six-to-one, or even three-to-one, ratio of positive to negative comments. Some days, my self-talk doesn't measure up to that ratio either. Most days.

Naturally, some people are more sensitive than others. Some hear a comment and take it at face value, while others attach deeper meaning to the words, analyzing them and worrying about the significance of the sender's message. They feel rejected and unloved. Some accept criticism readily, while others internalize a small critique and beat themselves up with negative thoughts about themselves.

The discussion about setting the dinner table is an example of a minor incident in our house. Many children reside in homes in which most sentences they hear are harsh and mean. Their caregivers tell them they will never amount to anything, that they are burdens, that they cost too much money and take too much time. Parents or guardians scold them for every minor transgression or completely ignore them.

As we grow up, we form opinions of ourselves based on our surroundings. At one time or another, we look at our physical makeup or an intrinsic trait and decide we don't like what we see or who we are. We compare our weaknesses to our neighbor's strengths and believe that we aren't hitting the mark, that we are subpar, less than average, and not normal. These sentiments can compile. However we arrive at our feelings of rejection, insecurity, and inadequacy, be it through a direct message, an indirect message, or internal thoughts, if we don't detect the emotions manifesting as self-doubt and attend to them, our behavior will reflect our negative thoughts about ourselves.

> We compare our weaknesses to our neighbor's strengths and believe that we aren't hitting the mark, that we are subpar, less than average, and not normal.

It boils down to identity. Who do we believe we are? Whose do we believe we are?

When we put our faith in Jesus Christ, we are made new. "Just as Christ was raised from the dead through the glory of the Father, we too may live a new life" (Rom. 6:4).

No Relationship with Christ
That brings us to the next component in our equation. Let's look at it again:

self-doubt + no relationship with Christ + everyone's doing it = a perpetual cycle of unhealthy relationships

My grandparents' generation attended church every time the doors were open. Besides the guilt factor—*we might rot in hell if we don't go to church at least once per week*—church was a hub for social interaction. Community halls, backyards, and the church were the hotspots for events. My parents' generation, the baby boomers, rebelled against the assumption that attending church magically made you a good person, and they let their kids make their own choices regarding religion. Accordingly, we have seen a decline in church attendance and religious affiliation with each new generation, so much so that when completing a questionnaire, a new category of religion is available: "none."

A few years ago, my pastor husband asked a group of kids at an after-school event who Jesus was. One boy said he'd never heard of him. Unfortunately, this isn't an isolated incident. Because of the trend over the past half century for teens to walk away from the church when they are old enough to "think for themselves," we now have parents who don't attend church or read the Bible at home. Thus, our young children don't know who Jesus Christ is.

Because the number of those who don't adhere to Christian principles or walk with Christ is rising, they, as a group, have a greater influence on society and cultural norms. Hence, a culture in which casual sex before marriage is normal, and Christians who frown on this behavior are few and far between.

Many children, preteens, teens, and young adults don't have a relationship with Christ simply because they haven't been told who he is. So they search for love, acceptance, and a sense of belonging outside of God. What they find through peers, media, and family is hollow and disappointing.

Everyone's Doing It

self-doubt + no relationship with Christ + everyone's doing it = a perpetual cycle of unhealthy relationships

Peer pressure is real, and perception is reality. Even I feel it. My husband and I went on a middle-of-the-winter four-day get-away to an all-inclusive hotel in Mexico one year because two of my friends went with their husbands. I didn't want to be left out. I enjoyed my vacation but concluded that the expense wasn't worth what turned out to be an enormous hassle—think ice storm and twenty-four hours in an airport—for a brief stay. But I can process decisions logically and exercise self-control when tempted by beautifully photographed scenery on my friends' social media accounts. Our children are more likely to succumb to the pull.

The pressure students experience in middle school, high school, and college is colossal and burdensome. They endure ridicule and face being outcast if they dress incorrectly, don't respond to texts in a timely manner, or use an improper filter on their social media photos. And trends are shifting at a faster pace than ever. The most popular social media app two years ago is now in the graveyard, having been exchanged for a newer, better model. It's hard to keep up, but no one wants to be in the dark or left behind.

People learn innately by observing and imitating. Students are fed information all day long through media, conversation, and surveying their surroundings. They trust what they read and see, especially if it's confirmed by their peers. They absorb this information through the lens of previous experiences and interactions, and they make assumptions, which sometimes leads to faulty conclusions. Then they imitate what they see, and they are motivated by fear of missing out (FOMO) or being rejected.

In hookup culture, the definition of a hookup is purposefully vague so students can give the illusion of having sex when, in reality, they may be only kissing, possibly having intercourse, or something in between. But, if someone new to the circle—and sometimes new is simply being a freshman on campus—hears that a high percentage of classmates are hooking up and confirms this data by scrolling through social media, the student is inclined to seek a partner for casual sex just to fit in. Otherwise, the student may face teasing and mockery. Never mind the fact that plenty of students are choosing not to engage in hookups.

Pornography promotes hookup culture by falsely portraying sex as rough, spontaneous, and emotionally void. Women are treated as objects and commodities. Unfortunately, porn is now where children turn for their sex education. When putting porn and hookup culture together, teens not only believe that everyone is doing *it*, but they think everyone is doing it *this way*. These thoughts are confirmed through games and movies.

> When putting porn and hookup culture together, teens not only believe that everyone is doing *it*, but they think everyone is doing it *this way*.

A Perpetual Cycle of Unhealthy Relationships

We've now arrived at the other side of the equation:

self-doubt + no relationship with Christ + everyone's doing it = a perpetual cycle of unhealthy relationships

The components on the left side of the equation add up to a string of superficial relationships. I hesitate to use the word *relationships* because many of these meetups or online exchanges are more like contractual interactions without the contract.

The cycle starts in middle school. Sending nudes replaced saying hello. It's the precursor to dating. Girls are teased if no one has requested a nude from them yet. That's a lot of pressure.

The adults in their lives may be coaching them, bolstering them, or trying to help them understand their worth. Or their parents, grandparents, or guardians could be oblivious to the environment, not realizing the need to counterbalance what children hear and see at school. Either way, the weight to fit in is heavy, making it easier to ignore an adult's warnings and cave to the influence of peers, especially at that age. Once preteens or teens compromise, they are more apt to progress to the next level. They may believe they are exercising independence and guiding their own destiny, but they're actually being swayed by their surroundings.

We can also assume they're experiencing thoughts and feelings of inadequacy, insecurity, and self-doubt. Because their brain isn't developed, they not only can't predict how their current actions will affect their future, but they're unable to decipher why these decisions aren't making them feel better about themselves. This starts a chain of events that condition their propensity toward certain actions, like seeking acceptance and worth through relationships, as they mature into adulthood.

The cycle may not begin in middle school; it could start later. Without a solid foundation built on who God says they are, preteens, teens, or young adults end up in a series of unhealthy relationships with no insight as to why they aren't finding long-term fulfillment. Without a trusted adult alongside them pointing to the potential physical and emotional dangers of online encounters and a casual-sex mentality, they don't know how to find and maintain a healthy relationship.

I was talking with a colleague about hookup culture. She's divorced and a single mom of a middle school student. During our conversation, she told me how difficult it is to find someone willing to go out before hooking up, which confirms the widespread belief that casual sex is a prerequisite to dating.[2] These principles are so ingrained in society that even my coworker, a Christian woman committed to searching for that special someone with her same values, morals, and biblical foundation, has a hard time finding a companion.

Repercussions

What is the fallout of these beliefs and actions? What are the ramifications and outcomes of a society living for constant dopamine hits? What are the negative repercussions of this lifestyle?

I was presenting on the influence of media at a high school. I asked a student to put her phone away. She set it on the table in front of her. Three minutes later, I asked her to put her phone away again. She set it down again. I stated, "Teens are on screens an average of nine hours per day, outside of schoolwork. During those nine hours, they see four thousand ads. Do you think that much media influences you? Do you think seeing four thousand advertisements a day impacts you?" When I looked up, this gal was scrolling on her phone. I called on her to answer a question, and she didn't hear me. I don't think she even realized she'd picked up her phone—again.

Students watch movies, play games, listen to music, post on social media, and text all day long, at least in some of the schools my team and I visit. It was problematic before COVID-19. Now it's excessive.

But they aren't alone. I do it, too. I find myself mindlessly checking my phone every ten minutes. I don't even know why. I check the time. I check the weather. I look to see if anyone liked my latest post. I feel lost without the phone in my possession, and I panic a little when I can't find it.

To further my point about how many hours we look at screens each day, I asked this same class, "How many of you check your phone between classes?" They almost all raised their hands. One guy volunteered, "I look at it 'cause I'm bored." Yes! Their brains (mine too?) are so used to constant stimulation that when they face a few minutes of downtime, they need to fill the space.

Neither Gen Z nor Generation Alpha have lived in a period of no cell phones. Even if they didn't own one in their early development years, their parents did. They are conditioned to keep their brains busy and at a fast pace. They aren't learning how to slow down, to be still, to relax and allow their minds and bodies to unwind. They don't know how to sit quietly with their own thoughts. And that's detrimental to their well-being.

Ramifications on Individuals

Ramifications of these societal norms have trickled down to Gen Z and Generation Alpha. They are the ones innocently affected because, in general, they don't know better. But persons of all ages show wear-and-tear signs and experience negative consequences. Even though people are more connected than ever, they are lonelier than ever. Social media has not fulfilled our desire to bond and belong. Instead, it has isolated us, caused us to compare ourselves more, and intensified FOMO, the fear of missing out. This fear drives people to stay up all night texting, scrolling, and gaming. Then in the morning, they feel more uncertain than ever, not to mention sleep-deprived.

These behaviors have a cumulative effect. Sure, there are those who engage in hookups, pornography, and all-night gaming with no internal or external sign of aftermath, but most will experience some type of letdown and long-term issue. These touch all areas of life.

Physical

I've referred to one physical ramification, STDs. Some who participate in casual sex are concerned with catching an STD or producing an unwanted pregnancy. But prevention entails more than putting on a condom, as a sexually transmitted disease can spread through other types of sexual activity besides intercourse. This is such an issue that the Centers for Disease Control and Prevention says that the most reliable way to avoid sexually transmitted infections is to abstain from sex—vaginal, oral, and anal.

Erectile dysfunction can be a physical problem for men using pornography. A male dependent on porn may not be able to perform when trying to have sex. That's a deterrent you may want to pass along to your boys.

Then there is the possible bruising, choking, and damage to sexual organs caused by sexual abuse emulated in pornography and promoted in gaming and other online activities, such as browsing the Internet, scrolling social media accounts, and instant messaging.[3]

As time passes, other signs of distress on the body may include weight loss, weight gain, cancer, acid reflux, sleep deprivation, headaches, and other bodily manifestations associated with stress, anxiety, depression, and isolation.

Intellectual

We've explored how the brain modifies itself based on habits. Someone worried about fitting in could experience lapses in judgment or an altered state of intelligence. A student may be unable to focus on academics. An employee may fall short of an employer's standards. And a person's attention span may be shorter than the attention span of someone who is not distraught or on a screen constantly.

Emotional

People ensnared in this lifestyle may experience fear, worry, or heartbreak. When they no longer see themselves as worthy, loved, or valued, self-esteem plummets. They may feel numb, sad, or depressed. They could suffer regret, confusion, or a sense of loss. They may question their reason for existing. Often, these emotions lead to suicidal thoughts, a growing problem in teens.

Guilt and shame are two powerful emotions for those who struggle with a repeated issue or an addiction. Our children, like everyone, crave connection and a place to belong, but shame and guilt distort their perspective. They can't see the unconditional love and acceptance we're trying to communicate.

Pornography, an *as long as you're happy* perspective, and hookup culture project a false front. They imitate connection and deceive their targets into believing what they're selling will fulfill their inner desire to connect and belong. Our children fall into the trap. Once there, shame and guilt keep them isolated from the people who love them most.

> Pornography, an *as long as you're happy* perspective, and hookup culture project a false front.

When caregivers comprehend this cycle, their ability to safeguard their children improves. Our job as parents is to identify the gap between us and our children and to bridge that gap so we can better bond with them and help them. If you observe any of the above behaviors or sense that your child's emotions aren't normal, check in with your child. Talk about it, and offer help.

Spiritual

When we don't fully comprehend or value who we are in Christ, we may believe we are worthless and insignificant. Furthermore, what may be conviction and a sense of God calling us to him could be misinterpreted as shame.

Paul explains this dilemma in Romans. "So I find this law at work: Although I want to do good, evil is right there with me. For in my inner being I delight in God's law; but I see another law at work in me, waging war against the law of my mind and making me a prisoner of the law of sin at work within me" (Rom. 7:21–23). These back-and-forth battles lead to thoughts of insecurity and defeat. "What a wretched man I am! Who will rescue me from this body that is subject to death?" (Rom. 7:24). Unfortunately, many stop here, not realizing the answer is outside themselves or others. But Paul tells us the answer. "Thanks be to God, who delivers me through Jesus Christ our Lord!" (Rom. 7:25).

It comes back to identity. When we understand who we are in Christ, that we are priceless in God's eyes, we are less likely to fall into these traps and suffer from the consequences. And when we do find ourselves hurting from our decisions or the choices those around us have made, we still have hope.

Ramifications on Relationships

The fallout of this lifestyle goes beyond affecting individuals. While we brag about being an individualistic society and boast how certain actions don't hurt anyone else, in actuality, most decisions have a larger reach than we claim.

My son initially believed his pornography addiction didn't affect anyone besides himself. When his behavior was brought to light, it damaged our relationship. In addition to feeling as if I had wronged him and somehow broken him beyond repair, I felt betrayed. When the dust settled, the fact that he had disregarded my teachings, gone behind my back, and lied to me was more upsetting than his other choices. The trust between us was broken. I no longer believed what he told me. Once lack of trust enters a relationship, it's difficult to regain.

Lisa Wade, author of *American Hookup: The New Culture of Sex on Campus*, found that students engaging in hookup culture expect a stimulating and carefree life. Instead, they report their relationships have been traumatic, disillusioning, and deeply disappointing. They state that their sexual meetups are distressing. They are frustrated and regretful. And many say they have been sexually coerced or assaulted. The author discloses that hookup culture is dangerous for both the potential victim and potential assailant because the culture creates an environment in which students not only think they can coerce but that they should.[4]

When calloused and emotionless hookups or rough and violent sex have been the norm, understanding the importance of putting others first, acting kindly, and learning to foster a relationship is not easy or natural. Even one traumatic encounter can leave someone hollow, broken, and raw. Years of unhealthy interactions through hookups or short-term relationships cause emotional scars and bruises, inhibiting the ability to be intimate with another human being.

I lost my virginity at fifteen, but my first sexual experience was in elementary school. A friend laid next to me and put his hand on my breasts, or, rather, where breasts would eventually develop. I wouldn't have labeled it as a form of sexual activity, and I didn't object, but that occurrence stuck with me. I had multiple boy-friends through my middle school and high school years. Each left an imprint on me. When I think about the pain and the emotional ups and downs these relationships caused, I can see why hookup culture is appealing. If it were possible to be sexually satisfied with-out the stress and heartaches of new relationship drama, I'd think about it, too. Unfortunately, that claim is a lie. Whether we realize it or not, each encounter leaves an impression, positive or negative.

If we don't recognize the emotionally destructive signs and process them, we will carry the wounds into the next relation-ship. They will accumulate until our list of hurts, injuries, and insecurities far surpasses our list of skills, accomplishments, and confidences. I lugged all the wounds from each relationship into my first marriage. Then, after my divorce, I swapped some of those wounds for new ones. But the rejection wound—the one that said I wasn't good enough, loving enough, kind enough, sexy enough, whatever enough to keep a man—I carried into my second mar-riage. And it didn't stay hidden for long.

The fallout doesn't stay confined within a marriage or partner-ship relationship. No, it spills over into other relationships. When we think poorly of ourselves, that we don't measure up to stan-dards (our own or others'), or we have open wounds because we've been hurt or rejected, the aftereffect manifests itself in friendships, at work, within dating relationships, and in parenting. Before we know it, we're screaming at our kids because they spilled milk on the floor. We think we're mad because they can't hold a glass still. In reality, the spilled milk ignited the anger we'd been holding in. We're angry at ourselves or others, and it comes gushing out at the wrong person, the easy target.

Ramifications on Society

Over time, the effects of unhealthy relationships touch society. When we're around negative behaviors or lifestyles frequently, we become desensitized to wrongdoings and acclimate to our surroundings. People, especially children, mimic what they see modeled. When adults don't comprehend how to connect and bond with others in their circle of influence, the skill isn't passed on to the next generation.

> When adults don't comprehend how to connect and bond with others in their circle of influence, the skill isn't passed on to the next generation.

Technology is beneficial but has its drawbacks. We've moved toward a community that interacts via texts, quips, photos, and short video clips. We're accustomed to immediate and divisive feedback. We aren't allowing room for exploring topics or having deep, meaningful conversations. Therefore, we aren't relating as well in person. The conversation is more strained and doesn't leave room for differences of opinion. We are abrupt, impolite, and sometimes hostile. Or we're aloof and noncommittal. And we aren't willing to change our ways.

The digital age brought distractions. We no longer have to think or face our problems. We can occupy our minds with outside sources twenty-four hours a day if we want. Games and pornography blur the lines between fantasy and reality, altering brain function and confusing even those trying their best to live a good life.

The cumulative effect is a society that can't distinguish right from wrong or understand where their emotional turmoil comes from.

Unfortunately, the church isn't as influential as it once was. We've allowed societal norms to cloud our judgment and affect our decisions. We've ignored, we've remained ignorant, or we've come out swinging. In other words, those of us within the Christian circle are just as confused as everyone else about how to respond to the deterioration of relationships.

But we don't have to stay in this state of bewilderment. We can choose to make a difference. It takes intentionality, determination, research, and discussions. It takes reading God's Word and listening to the Holy Spirit. And it takes prayer—lots of prayer.

habits for healthy relationships

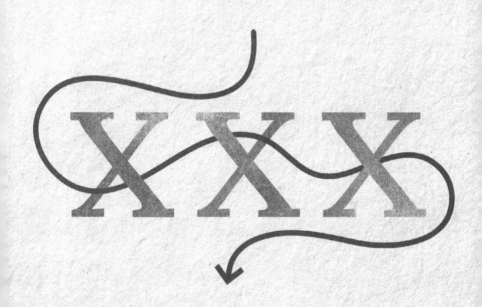

Love

See what great love the Father has lavished on us, that
we should be called children of God! (1 John 3:1)

I took seven steps toward the window, flipped my dress, and strode seven steps toward the chair. When I bumped into the chair, I picked up my train, threw it around, and retraced my steps back to the window. As I paced back and forth, I cried, mumbled, and blew my nose.

I'm sure I was quite the sight. I was nineteen and in my wedding dress—train, veil, puffy sleeves, and all—treading back and forth while talking to myself like a crazy woman. The tears weren't happy tears. They were irrational hormonal tears. Maybe the heat instigated the breakdown. The June weather brought another ninety-degree day. The drought was so bad my flowers arrived on ice. My bridesmaids and mother watched me fall apart. They were as clueless as I was about how to stop the emotional torrent pouring from my body. If one of them dared come near, I shooed her away.

I wasn't assessing my decision to marry, but my emotions were rebelling and betraying my reasoning. After all, this was a major commitment catapulting my life in a new direction, and it was problematic if it turned out to be a mistake.

Looking back, I question how much thought I put into my first engagement. Since I was leaving for college, it seemed like the logical decision, so we jumped in. That's not uncommon. Plenty of people marry young and enjoy a long and fulfilling life together. The odd part was that I believed, going in, that this would be my first marriage. I had a preconceived idea that marriages didn't last; therefore, this was my first marriage.

But why? My grandparents had stayed married until death did them part. Why would I assume marriages were disposable, not to be taken seriously? Was it because I didn't know Jesus, read the Bible, or follow his ways? Or because my bridegroom, who was standing at the altar and waiting for me to be presented to him by my father, and I had broken up multiple times in the years we'd been together? Or because I was so immersed in the culture that I had bought into the lie that relationships come and go, and that's okay? Or was it because I was young and naïve? I'm guessing it was a combination of all these.

If we take our cues from the news, movies, social media, and our peers (even our church friends), we may get an inaccurate picture of true love. Sensationalized romance, the love-at-first-sight and always-attracted-to-each-other type, sells. The ongoing, tedious, day-in-and-day-out, work-out-your-differences-and-through-your-conflicts type of love is boring and hard work.

Living with another fallible human is not appealing in this *as long as you're happy* instant-gratification culture.

> If we take our cues from the news, movies, social media, and our peers (even our church friends), we may get an inaccurate picture of true love.

Yet, we long for true love. Our minds, bodies, and souls crave deep, intimate, unconditional, long-lasting love. So, we seek. And when we're disappointed, we seek elsewhere. And then we seek again. When we come up empty, we blame ourselves or those around us.

But what if we're looking in the wrong places? What if we don't find love because we don't know where to search? What if no one has modeled a healthy relationship centered on God? I think that's the battle many millennials, Gen Zers, and members of Generation Alpha face. And we can't blame them. As we explored in Section One, relationships have been on a slow decline and have deteriorated for generations. This is partially due to techno-logical changes and disengagement from biblical principles over the years.

What does a healthy, loving relationship involve? Can we effectively help those behind us live a more fulfilling life? Are we able to steer the culture in a more positive direction? Is there hope for us and the next generation? Yes.

Understand the Culture

If we look at the book of Daniel in the Bible, we see our children aren't the first thrust into a strange world. Daniel and his friends lived in a time of turmoil. Foreigners snatched them from their homeland, forcing them to grow up in Babylon. These four young men, along with others, were handpicked to serve in the king's palace. Talk about pressure.

"The king assigned them a daily amount of food and wine from the king's table. They were to be trained for three years, and after that they were to enter the king's service" (Dan. 1:5). Daniel, not wanting to corrupt his body with food unsanctioned by God, asked the king's official for permission to eat only vegetables and drink only water.

A noteworthy point is that Daniel was not disrespectful or impolite. He approached the king's official with confidence but not arrogance. The official was afraid of the king, rightfully so, and didn't want to get in trouble—die—when these four looked like beanpoles next to the other boys because they weren't eating well. Daniel sympathized but didn't back down. He offered a compromise. "Please test your servants for ten days . . . Then compare our appearance with that of the young men who eat the royal food, and treat your servants in accordance with what you see" (Dan. 1:12–13). Daniel took the burden of proof on himself and relieved the official of any liability. How could he refuse? After the ten days, "they looked healthier and better nourished than any of the young men who ate the royal food" (Dan. 1:15).

Daniel took the time to get to know the official, the beliefs of the nation, and the behavior expected of him. He evaluated the situation, and even though he was forced to live within the culture, he chose not to conform to it. He resolved not to turn from God and subject himself to the king of this distant land. Fear did not control his decisions. He grew up studying and meditating on Scripture, and he trusted that God's ways were best.

Our culture is changing at a rapid pace. While sometimes it's hard to keep up, it's advantageous to understand the culture we live in. As parents, grandparents, and caregivers, inside and outside the church, we can educate ourselves on the dynamics and customs of the environment our children and grandchildren face every day— at school, at youth group, at their sporting events and after-school activities, and through their social interactions in person and online. We are more effective if we grasp the reality of our surroundings. Then we can come alongside our children from a place of compassion and guide them toward healthier relationships.

Be a Model

How do we initiate change? By starting at the ground level—within families, churches, and communities. By adhering to the principles we want our children to follow and modeling the behavior we hope for. The next generation is more apt to respond to our teaching when we live out values, morals, and biblical instructions.

Easier said than done. Some of us didn't grow up in a healthy environment. Some of us learned later in life how to interact with others in a loving, godly manner. And some of us are still wondering what a healthy relationship looks like. So, let's explore habits of a healthy relationship.

Foundation of a Healthy Relationship

If we picture a relationship as a structure, we recognize the need for a strong and sturdy foundation. Relationships with weak foundations will crumble. However, when a solid foundation is constructed, each brick, block, or wall added to the base will stay in place, keep the building square, and add to its beauty. And the building will stay upright long past our lifetime.

The foundation of a healthy relationship is Christlike love.

We flippantly use the word *love*. We say we love a sunset or we love a good steak. We talk about loving, or not loving, our job or our car. And, of course, we love our spouse, our parents, and our children. But defining love is not easy. Is *love* a noun or a verb? Is it based on a feeling or a decision? Is it permanent or provisional?

How does Scripture explain love? Let's look at a few passages to clarify its meaning. In 1 John, we learn "God is love" (1 John 4:16) and "This is love: not that we loved God, but that he loved us and sent his Son as an atoning sacrifice for our sins" (1 John 4:10). From these verses, we learn that God cannot be separated from love. If we know God, then we know love. Furthermore, because of his love, he sent Jesus as a sacrifice for our sins. Jesus also loves us and demonstrated it by laying his life down for us (see 1 John 3:16). This act illustrates the depth and devotion of Christ's love.

As humans, we get a sense of this, to a degree, when we think of the love we have for our children. Most parents would literally die to save their child. If we stop for a moment and visualize ourselves diving in front of a bullet headed toward our child's heart, we get a tiny glimpse of the dedication and desire Jesus had for us, his dying children, and his motivation for going to the cross.

Our children can get on our nerves. We may complain about problems that arise from taking care of others. We sometimes allow the longevity of parenting to get under our skin. But we would still take that bullet. When Jesus walked with his disciples from one town to the other, listened to them question his directions, and watched them bicker among themselves, he didn't see their childish behavior and ponder whether his upcoming sacrifice was worth it. No, he saw their hearts and stayed focused on the long-term goal. He knew these men and women were God's precious children who needed rescued.

Of course, we would take the bullet. Like Jesus, most of us would die for our children. But what about the days when loving requires other sacrifices, other demonstrations of love? Is our choice as easy? No. Making a snap decision to dive in front of a bullet is different than choosing to respond calmly when a child spills milk, needs a last-minute ride to a basketball game, or confesses he's been watching pornography. That's why God's love is essential. Without it, we are helpless and unable to love others well.

> Making a snap decision to dive in front of a bullet is different than choosing to respond calmly when a child spills milk, needs a last-minute ride to a basketball game, or confesses he's been watching pornography.

It's on the hard days, the ones when people are unlovable and treating us harshly, when our love is tested. Those are the days we choose love because the people around us, the very ones making our lives difficult, are God's creation, and he desires for us to show them his love. "Dear friends, since God so loved us, we also ought to love one another. No one has ever seen God; but if we love one another, God lives in us and his love is made complete in us" (1 John 4:11–12).

On our worst days, God loves us. On the days we've failed, made poor choices, hurt others, and sinned against him, he loves us categorically. He doesn't regret his decision to accept us into his family. He's not astonished by our behavior or insecurities or lack of maturity. He doesn't doubt creating us. No, he still sees us as chosen, holy, loved, blameless, forgiven, and redeemed. (See Ephesians 1:1–7.)

For us to love others unconditionally, we embrace these truths. We are only capable of loving others if we receive God's love first. "If anyone acknowledges that Jesus is the Son of God, God lives in them and they in God. And so we know and rely on the love God has for us" (1 John 4:15–16). When we rely on God's love, we trust him by leaning into him and leaning on him with the expectation that he will be there and will keep us from falling. Relying means putting faith in him and depending on him without a contingency plan.

"We love because he first loved us" (1 John 4:19). True love, unrestricted love, a long-lasting love, originates from the love imbedded within us by God himself. Without it, our words and actions fall short. Our motives aren't pure. Our interactions lack integrity. Knowing God and living by his Spirit produces an inspired, sincere, and hope-filled love. When we love our children with the love God placed in our hearts for them, they sense it. They listen to our advice because they trust our motives.

It comes back to modeling the behavior and principles we hope to encourage in the next generation. If we desire for them to have healthy relationships, maybe we should ask ourselves if we are in healthy relationships. The first relationship to examine, the one at the core of all the others, is the relationship we have with Christ.

Depend on God First

When I was nineteen and walking down the aisle during a drought in the puffy-sleeved white dress with the train, I didn't know Jesus. In fact, the church I chose for my wedding was the one in our small town that sat the most guests. I find that comical now. My lack of familiarity with Jesus wasn't necessarily the reason the marriage failed, but it didn't help.

When I met my current husband, Don, we were both recently divorced and each raising a son. Neither of us was actively looking for someone to date, much less a potential spouse, so we were skittish about getting involved. We cautiously started talking while trying to judge the other one's character. I was recovering from a yearlong separation that ended in divorce, and I was juggling a new career and learning how to be a single mom.

In the years between my first wedding and my divorce, I met Jesus and nurtured my relationship with him. I read my Bible faithfully, prayed, attended church, and matured in my faith. The year I was separated was a bittersweet year. My heart broke, but my love for Jesus and my trust in him grew exponentially. I learned to depend on him as my bridegroom and provider. He walked with me and beside me. He met me in the darkest places. He comforted me and uplifted me. He used others to show me his love, and he met my needs in ways that can only be described as miraculous.

Don had been through a similar experience. Even though he knew Christ when he first married, his relationship with him grew during the years he was married to his first wife, separated, and then divorced. Don knew the importance of a solid connection with God. We both had learned how to transfer our dependence from a former spouse to our all-knowing, all-powerful God.

Don and I met through a mutual friend. She told me he worked long hours and needed a babysitter in the evenings temporarily. Since our sons attended the same daycare, she thought it would be convenient for me to watch him.

Our friend passed my number to Don. He called that evening to inquire if I could pick up his son the next day. I said yes, and he asked to drop by my apartment for his son to meet me. While his safety concerns impressed me, I was a bit aggravated because I was putting my son to bed. I agreed, thinking I would answer the door, give a quick greeting to his child, and get back to my nighttime routine. It didn't quite go as I planned.

When I opened the door, a tall, handsome man filled my doorframe. I said hello. To my dismay, he stepped into my home without an invitation and sat on my couch. Alarms went off in my head. *Single guy in the house. Single guy in the house.* I was frantic and intrigued at the same time. I wasn't sure if I should call the police or offer him a cup of coffee. Thankfully, he wasn't a serial killer. The conversation went well and ended quickly.

Over the next several weeks, while I watched his son, Don and I became friends. He joined the single parent group at my church, and we frequently hung out at activities sponsored by the group. Before long, we were talking for hours on the phone and learning each other's likes and dislikes, history and future goals, and current beliefs. We analyzed our first marriages and their downfalls. We chatted about the brokenness of divorce and the difficulty of healing and recovering. When he worked up the nerve to ask me out, I told him I wasn't dating until I had spent time alone to allow Christ to restore me. This declaration didn't deter him. He was impressed with my promise to Christ and desire to seek him first. (Don would tell you that's the moment he realized he wanted to marry me.)

During one of our long discussions, we contemplated how couples interact. Our conclusion? When broken people hop into relationships eager to fix the other person or to be fixed, the new couple has a high chance of failure. For an optimal relationship, one that starts strong and remains healthy, each person needs to be independently dependent on God first. Each should feel complete and be able to survive apart from others, relying solely on God, before pursuing someone else. Otherwise, the relationship becomes more about receiving and filling a felt need rather than giving and offering from what God provides.

When someone comes to a relationship depleted and needy, the bond is weak from the beginning. It can certainly recover, but it will take effort and a willingness by both parties to identify and conquer the issues.

A question hung on the wall of the counselor I saw during my separation: *Are you functioning from acceptance or for acceptance?* On days I fall into the trap of seeking love from others, I go back to this question. When we allow God to fill us with his love and acceptance, we subsequently love others well because his love overflows from us to those around us. But when we attempt to obtain love through someone else, be it a friend, spouse, parent, or child, we will be disappointed. Whomever we rely on to satisfy our longings will fall short.

Another Wedding Day

Six months after meeting Don, I stood in my straight-lined wedding dress near the church window and surveyed the thick snowflakes falling from the sky. Two feet had piled up, and the storm threatened to go all night. I had arrived an hour earlier with a shopping bag over my head to protect my updo and hair piece made of fresh flowers. I watched the snowplow attempt to clear the parking lot and prayed for the guests who would brave the blizzard to witness Don and me exchange vows.

The roads were so treacherous that two members of the wedding party, out-of-town family, chose not to attend. When they asked about our plan B, we said there wasn't one—we were getting married despite the conditions. Last minute stand-ins were chosen the day before.

Typically, these unforeseen circumstances would tip my emotions into overdrive, but not this day. Unlike my first wedding, a peace washed over me. As I walked down the aisle toward that tall handsome man who had filled my doorframe and set off alarms in my head the first time we met, my heart filled with joy.

The ceremony would be poorly attended, and our van would slip and slide twenty miles through snow drifts to the bed-and-breakfast, but I was content. The wedding itself wasn't the main event; the marriage was. As I thought of our upcoming life together, I smiled and anticipated the new adventure God had asked me to begin.

Our decision to marry felt right. We had, individually and as a couple, leaned on God and sought his will. We were convinced this marriage was sanctioned by him, and we were taking a leap of faith. Besides, we hadn't only fallen in love; we had become best friends.

A Durable Foundation

Neither Don nor I wanted to be the other one's savior. We knew we couldn't enter a relationship in which either would be put on a pedestal or seen as a rescuer. That type of reliance or idolization would lead to heartache and distress. We recognized our human nature and lack of ability and power to change someone else, or even help them, if that person wasn't first depending on God to supply their needs.

That doesn't mean our marriage was miraculously flawless from day one. Two single parents with ex-spouses and years of life behind them drag baggage, insecurities, and issues into their new life. We understood marriages contain laughter and tears, play and work, victory and tragedy. Life has ups and downs, and neither of us could shield the other from whatever problems and issues were in front of us. But we had a sound foundation of faith and trust in God to build on. Periodically, we removed a few bricks in our structure. We tore down a wall or two that was built in haste. We even called in some professionals for help every now and then. But the foundation remained durable.

Deep wounds don't heal easily, and habits aren't detected and remedied quickly. We had ours. You probably have yours. And our children and grandchildren have theirs, too. Understanding who we are in Christ, regularly relinquishing control to him, and receiving his love and acceptance is imperative. Otherwise, those hurts spill over onto others.

Actions Affect Others

In Chapter One, we investigated the *as long as they're happy* attitude. Sometimes an extra phrase accompanies this opinion. I've heard this variation: *as long as they're happy and healthy.* And then there's this one: *as long as they're happy and not hurting anyone else.* This particular expression encompasses a well-known belief that it's possible to make choices without affecting anyone else. It's a reasonable conclusion, especially post-pandemic. Many of us work from home, shop from home, and interact with coworkers, friends, and family from home. We are independent, consult no one, and make our own choices. Therefore, we presume our deeds have no residual effects and don't touch others.

But no one exists in a vacuum. Our choices, big and small, affect others.

> No one exists in a vacuum. Our choices,
> big and small, affect others.

If teens avoid fruits and vegetables and eat only chocolate chip ice cream and Fruity Pebbles, they may experience headaches, fatigue, and heart disease as adults. We could assume these symptoms only affect the ones who skipped the salad bar at lunch, but a tired employee isn't productive, and a cranky parent yields not-so-cheerful children.

Even a one-time event, like stealing a pen from an employer, could make a difference, especially if five hundred employees think their one-time pen-stealing heist doesn't amount to anything. At one dollar per pen, the employees robbed their employer of five hundred dollars.

Certainly, there are exceptions. When a single gal purchases yellow towels rather than baby blue, the decision may not impact anyone else. But who knows? Those bright towels may lighten her mood. If, after using said towels, she dashes into the gas station for a latte, her smile could alter the attendant's disposition for the day. The chain reaction is immeasurable.

But there are more serious consequences to our choices. A seemingly simple hookup involves a minimum of two people. Each has emotional, physical, and spiritual attachments or detachments. And while both may pretend their actions aren't influencing the other, their bodies' responses say otherwise.

A teen may believe watching pornography alone at night isn't affecting anyone else. Even if she feels guilt and shame along with the excitement porn induces, she probably thinks her deeds don't concern others. Unfortunately, that's not the case.

The majority of "actors" in pornographic videos didn't wake up one morning and resolve to become porn stars. They aren't fulfilling a lifelong dream. Most were coerced, bribed, deceived, or extorted into the business.[1] The pornography industry fuels the sex trafficking industry, and the sex trafficking industry fuels the pornography industry.[2] Explaining this link to the next generation is important for two reasons. First, they are susceptible to online grooming, extortion, and coercion. Second, when they comprehend that the choices they make in their own bedrooms affect other people—that their decisions may harm others—they may alter their decisions.

No one exists on an island. It's futile to believe that our actions don't have ripple effects. We respond in a loving manner to the world around us, to the cashier at the grocery store, or to the child within our home when we prioritize our relationship with Christ and allow him to fill us with his love. "We love because he first loved us" (1 John 4:19).

God's Love Never Fails

Functioning from acceptance means God's love fills us and, subsequently, overflows to others. Humans are created to commune and interact. Our souls long to love and be loved. We thrive by connecting. And the healthiest connections are those in which we receive God's love first and then allow that love to spill onto others.

What does God's love entail? Let's consider 1 Corinthians 13, often coined the "love chapter" of the Bible. This passage explains God's love for us and how to show his love to others.

Paul confirms for us at the beginning of the chapter that our words, offerings, and deeds are nothing without the foundation of Christlike love.

> If I speak in the tongues of men or of angels, but do not have love, I am only a resounding gong or a clanging cymbal. If I have the gift of prophecy and can fathom all mysteries and all knowledge, and if I have a faith that can move mountains, but do not have love, I am nothing. If I give all I possess to the poor and give over my body to hardship that I may boast, but do not have love, I gain nothing. (1 Cor. 13:1–3)

Healthy relationships are built on love, and God is love. Therefore, we lean into God to receive his love before beginning a new relationship or working on current ones. But how do we cultivate those relationships? What are the specifics? We'll turn to the rest of the passage to help us.

> Love is patient, love is kind. It does not envy, it does not boast, it is not proud. It does not dishonor others, it is not self-seeking, it is not easily angered, it keeps no record of wrongs. Love does not delight in evil but rejoices with the truth. It always protects, always trusts, always hopes, always perseveres.
>
> Love never fails. But where there are prophecies, they will cease; where there are tongues, they will be stilled; where there is knowledge, it will pass away. For we know in part and we prophesy in part, but when completeness comes, what is in part disappears. When I was a child, I talked like a child, I thought like a child,

I reasoned like a child. When I became a man, I put the ways of childhood behind me. For now we see only a reflection as in a mirror; then we shall see face to face. Now I know in part; then I shall know fully, even as I am fully known.

And now these three remain: faith, hope and love. But the greatest of these is love. (1 Cor. 13:4–13)

We will use this passage as the basis for the rest of the book, diving into specific habits of healthy relationships and mending ones not so healthy. As we move forward, let's remember that love never fails. People come and go, circumstances rise and fall, emotions hurl us into highs or lows, but God's love is constant and never-failing. He loves us as we are and will never stop loving us. That's a promise we can return to over and over.

> God's love is constant and never-failing.

CHAPTER

4

Selflessness

*Do nothing from selfish ambition or conceit, but in
humility count others more significant than yourselves.
Let each of you look not only to his own interests, but
also to the interests of others. (Phil. 2:3–4 ESV)*

Don and I ushered our son into this world on another snowy day two years after walking down that aisle. Our marriage had already endured hardships, including a miscarriage, so we were grateful to celebrate a new baby. We assumed our family was complete.

Entering adulthood, I wanted two children. I wasn't the mothering type, but when Don and I merged our small families, each bringing a boy into the mix, we agreed to add one more. I hoped for a girl, but I released that desire the day our son was born.

Several years later, God resurrected my dream for a girl when he called us to adopt. After we brought our daughter home, I overheard a relative say, "Now they have his, hers, ours, and theirs." I was sensitive and protective about my family and its formation. This impolite statement hurt me. I realize now she meant the comment as an explanation, not a judgment. Our circumstances have a unique quality to them, but isn't every family unique to a degree?

Each child God added to my home, he added to my heart. Each brought trials and joys, tears and laughter, failures—lots of failures—and triumphs. Each burrowed his or her way into my life and my soul. And each chiseled away at the selfish parts.

A child can bring out a parent's innermost ugliness like no one else, causing us to face our own weaknesses, flaws, and limitations. Parenting is the most grueling and inspiring job in the world. We are to lay our own wants, desires, and, at times, needs aside to take care of these beautiful creatures who depend on us for every little thing. I can think of no love outside of God that causes a person to relinquish selfishness as much as love for a child.

> Parenting is the most grueling and inspiring job in the world.

Our babies rely on us for life-sustaining food and shelter. Our toddlers require physical protection so they don't harm themselves. As our children grow and interact with friends and teachers, they need our guidance in the ways of the world.

When they reach the preteen and teen years, they count on our money—and so much more. Our role is to remind them they are not alone, while keeping our distance. This is difficult terrain. Each child is an individual with distinct necessities. And, try as we might, we can't always predict their requirements or responses to their environment.

Fourteen years after I birthed our baby boy that snowy day, I learned of his pornography habit. Having been a mom for twenty years, along with all the everyday moments and joyous occasions, I'd walked with my children through injuries, botched relationships, and emotional turmoil. I had held their hands through hurts, heartaches, and rejection. I had cried with them and for them. But nothing prepared me for this news. I felt like a failure, and I wanted to escape.

Unlike other relationships, ones with friends, coworkers, or even extended family, I couldn't walk away from my son. When I wanted to throw up because of his indiscretions, I still loved him. When I wanted to quit because parenting was too hard, I leaned into God and loved my son through another day. When I felt ignorant, unequipped, and useless, I fell to my knees.

At sixteen, my son confessed he was still using pornography. We learned he was addicted. I couldn't focus. My emotions, ever present, clouded my judgment. I teetered between uselessness and solving the problem by researching, talking, and taking charge. I lay in my bed crying my eyes out one minute and was ready to fight my son's battles the next. One thing I knew: I could not abandon him. Even if I said and did all the wrong things, even if I was screaming on the inside and hating our situation, I would persevere. My resolve to walk beside him and help him through his decision to quit required an inner strength I didn't know existed.

"Have a child," they said. "It'll be fun," they said. What they *didn't* say is how hard parenting is. How tedious. How long of an endeavor. How it turns your insides to mush because your child has stomped on your heart one day and the next made you proud as a peacock.

But parenting, if we allow it, also refines us. Parenting reminds us that life is not all about us. God uses our children to show us that our joys and delights originate from him. He uses outside experiences and people, especially our children, to draw us to him, where true love begins—a selfless love.

Types of Love

Ancient Greeks used multiple words to describe love, recognizing that expressions of love for people can be differentiated based on our connection with them. To understand the selfless love God shows us and asks us to extend to others, let's consider four of these words and their distinctions.

Eros

Eros denotes a passionate love, a love that is characterized by infatuation with someone else. Eros is based on hormonal instinct. Eros is sensual, intense, and often romantic. If someone were lusting after another and said they were in love, we'd say they were describing an eros love. In its purest form, meaning unaccompanied by another type of love, eros is inwardly focused, conditional, and specifically about the one experiencing the desire. This person is more interested in having her needs met than meeting those of the other. Eros is the root of the English word *erotic*.

We expect to find eros within a marriage. But it should accompany other types of love, specifically agape, which we will discuss in a moment. Healthy relationships include passion, physical attraction, and desire. Because of the hormones and chemicals at work in our brains and within our bodies, helping preteens and teens identify the difference between eros and other types of love is important.

Philia

Philia is an emotional bond without romantic feelings. This love involves respect, care, and compassion for others. Philia is common among friends and strengthens between them as they share their beliefs, values, and experiences. Philia is often referred to as brotherly love and is the root word of Philadelphia, the city of brotherly love in Pennsylvania.

Philia is typically what we think of when we talk about the love we have for each other within the church. Paul referred to this type of love in Romans when he said, "Be devoted to one another in brotherly love" (Rom. 12:10 NASB). The English Standard Version reads this way: "Love one another with brotherly affection."

Healthy relationships, especially between friends, but also within a marriage, experience philia. This type of attraction connects us and enhances our desire to spend time with others.

Storge

This lesser-known term describes familial love, the love we have for our children and family. Storge is built on memories and time spent together. Storge conveys a form of security we experience when surrounded by those who know us well, put up with our flaws, and still welcome us into their lives.

Agape

Called the highest form of love, agape is sacrificial and giving. It's never-ending and not based on the other person's performance or achievements. This is the love God displays and shows to humans, as evidenced by him sending his Son. Jesus showed agape by dying for us. His divine love is pure, selfless, and immeasurable. Agape is irrational. Agape surpasses emotions—agape is a determination to love, no matter the circumstances. Someone who demonstrates agape is motivated by the other person's best interest. Agape is given freely, with no expectations.

The Good Samaritan showed agape love to the man robbed on his way to Jericho. Jesus tells us in Luke 10:30–37 that the Samaritan was not dissuaded by the man's battered state or the inconvenience of a detour. Instead, he showed compassion and mercy by sacrificially providing for the man lying helpless on the ground. He stopped and stooped to assess the situation. He fulfilled the man's immediate needs, and he then continued to assist him by lifting him onto his donkey and transporting him to an inn. He followed through by paying for extra expenses and promising to return with more money, as needed. The Good Samaritan was interested in the full restoration of the hurt man. He used his God-given talents, abilities, and resources to pour into this stranger, demonstrating that love for a neighbor goes deeper than surface needs.

We learned in Chapter Three that God is love (agape); therefore, this love comes from God and God alone. Without him, we cannot understand, possess, or exhibit this type of love.

Healthy relationships include this selfless love. We hope marriages include eros, philia, and storge, but agape should be the foundation. Love for our children usually begins with agape love. Other types will follow. When interacting with friends, agape strengthens philia.

Distinguishing agape from philia, storge, and eros helps us analyze our relationships and helps us inspire the next generation to examine their relationships for signs of agape and other types of love.

We learn in the "love chapter," 1 Corinthians 13, that love—the word used here is *agape*—is selfless. "It does not dishonor others, it is not self-seeking, it is not easily angered, it keeps no record of wrongs. Love does not delight in evil but rejoices with the truth"

(1 Cor. 13:5–6). These are lofty goals and are impossible to achieve without God's love flowing through us.

We express selflessness by focusing on other people's needs and longings and by actively loving each person by considering their desires, dreams, goals, and wants.

> We express selflessness by focusing on other people's needs and longings and by actively loving each person by considering their desires, dreams, goals, and wants.

Needs and Longings

"Mom! Mom!" I opened my eyes to a dark room, my dream interrupted by someone calling me. "Mom! I'm sick!" My brain told my body to get up. I swung my legs over the side of the bed, paused, and stood. I threw on my robe and started praying as I headed down the hall.

My ten-year-old son sat on his bed with his trash can under his chin, a trick I'd taught him years before. "What's the matter?"

"I keep throwing up. I'm sorry to wake you. I don't know what to do." Even in my sleepy state, I smiled at his thoughtfulness.

"It's okay, honey. Of course, I want you to wake me." I sat next to him and put my hand on his forehead. It wasn't warm. "Tell me what you're feeling."

"My stomach hurts really bad."

He hopped up, ran to the bathroom, and knelt at the toilet. I followed and knelt next to him. Visions of him fainting in my arms years earlier invaded my thoughts. I pushed them out of the way so I could concentrate on his current needs. His stomach was in overdrive, trying to expel all manner of wretchedness, but there didn't appear to be much left. I suspected his nervousness had taken over. He was starting to panic, and his fear added to his troubled digestive system.

While lightly massaging his back, I spoke to him in hushed tones. "It's all right. Take some deep breaths through your nose."

When we made it back to his room, I prayed and put peppermint oil on his abdomen and lower back. My body ached for sleep, but my son's emotions hadn't settled.

"Will you stay with me until I fall asleep?"

"Sure. Why don't you roll over, and I'll rub your back."

I laid next to him. "How was your day?" he asked.

"I started a new book. You'd like it." I gave him a synopsis.

"It sounds interesting."

"Would you like me to read some of it to you?" I asked.

"Sure."

I grabbed the book from my nightstand and read for half an hour before he fell asleep.

My children rarely wake me. The two with weak stomachs have vomited in the middle of the night and told me the next day. This atypical incident stands out to me not because I was angry or fearful but because the memory is endearing. I cherish it because of the tender moments we shared. My son required more from me than physical care. He needed his mommy to sit with him, and despite my body's aching for sleep, I was available to supply his emotional and psychological needs. It was my privilege to be there for him.

The next morning during church, he wrote me a note, accompanied by a drawing of a mother sitting next to a child lying in bed. "If you're sick when you're old, I will sit by your bed until you fall asleep. Thank you."

We all have needs, the most basic of which are food, water, shelter, and clothing. Our bodies demand sleep and air to breathe, but our requirements go beyond these primal substances. God created us with other necessities—to thrive, not just survive. We aren't made simply to exist from one day to the next. We're meant to flourish, to give and receive, to consume and contribute.

What are these other needs? And why don't we give them the status they're meant to have? It's true that without water and food, our bodies will waste away. But without our longings met, we spiral into addiction, depression, or a sense of hollowness. Without connection and purpose, our existence appears meaningless.

Love and Acceptance

Each of us longs to feel loved and accepted as we are. God placed these innate desires within us so we would run to him and seek fulfillment from him.

As we explored in Chapter Three, our children learn to depend on God to meet these needs by observing us depend on God. We then display how to meet these needs in others by meeting them in our children's lives—loving and accepting them as they are. Sticking by them and bolstering them when they take a different path than we would choose for them. Expressing our love when they make a mistake, and saying we love them when they make illogical decisions.

Safety and Security

We yearn to feel safe and secure. When I lay my head on my pillow at night, I want to know no one will invade my home while I'm sleeping. I hope our jobs are secure so money is available to purchase food and clothing for the family. But I also long for my relationships, especially the one with my husband, to be safe and secure physically and emotionally. Don and I don't always agree, but I know he won't hurt me or leave me. This permits me to be myself within the confines of our marriage. I'm not frightened or fretting about pleasing him. This peace of mind wasn't instantaneous, however. Because of past relationships, we've both worked hard to reassure the other of our unconditional love, acceptance, and willingness to put effort into the relationship so it won't dissolve.

Our children need to trust they are safe and secure. Our job is to provide them with the peace of mind that comes with knowing there's another meal coming, a bed to sleep in, and a trusted adult available when they're scared or troubled. The ache for safety and security is not a perk or a privilege. It's not an added bonus. It's God-given. Our children may not grasp their desire for safety, consolation, and comfort within a relationship. Nonetheless, it exists, and we should address it. If we don't meet this longing, they will search for it elsewhere.

Sometimes, at an early age, our children experience a trauma that disrupts their needs from being met. A sibling dies, or parents divorce. Dad loses his job, and the family moves in with grandparents. While *we* understand our children are still safe physically and can bring their problems to us, the distress they've suffered leaves a permanent mark, causing them to feel insecure and unsafe and to possibly distrust everyone. The signs may not be visible. Some children, not wanting to be an extra burden, shield parents from emotional pain.

Reassure your children by listening, acknowledging their emotions, and telling them you will provide for them. Remind them that family problems are yours to solve, not theirs.

Belonging

We want to belong, to be included, to be part of something larger than ourselves—a community. We fulfill this pressing need by joining clubs, organizations, and churches. We attend concerts, parties, and community activities. We go to coffee with friends and attend Bible studies. We participate on social media.

Our children, likewise, wish to be part of the clique chitchat before class begins. They want to be invited to the lunch table by like-minded peers. They're hurt when their friends exclude them from group chats or texts. Fulfilling this need isn't optional. If our children's cravings to belong aren't met at home, they're more susceptible to peer pressure. Still, there's no guarantee they won't succumb to their friends' badgering. In our children's zeal to be included, they may follow peers into risky behaviors.

The aim is to create a space that fosters a sense of belonging within our homes and families. I admit, when my children were younger, I didn't always promote an environment that said, "You belong here." But seeing and meeting others' needs is fundamental to selfless love. This requires intentionality. Include them in conversations and decisions regarding family activities. Confirm that their contributions are accepted, desired, and helpful to the family dynamics.

Validation

We crave validation. This is big for me. I dislike being ignored or dismissed. I was shy as a child, and when I worked up the nerve to state my case, I felt rejected if my idea was disregarded, so I'd revert to being a person who didn't speak. As an adult, I've wrestled with when and how to express my ideas. At times, I've thought my opinions weren't valued because I was a woman. But that's a different book.

I've often told my husband, who is also my pastor, "I don't mind if you don't like my idea. However, I want to know you've heard me and considered my suggestions and my feelings before deciding. Please acknowledge I spoke and offer some feedback to indicate you understood my message. You'll get my buy-in quicker, and I'll be more pleasant to be around if my thoughts and emotions are validated."

We validate our children by looking them in the eye, listening to their words, repeating what we hear back to them, and affirming them. Say something positive about an idea they've expressed. Tell them you've heard them when they voice concerns. Remind them their emotions are real when they vent.

We can take all these steps and still disagree or make a choice contrary to their request. Validation is not the same as agreeing with an idea or believing emotions need nurtured. Sometimes we can't implement their ideas. Sometimes, feelings, although great indicators, are based on false perceptions and irrational thoughts. Confirm that the emotions exist, but steer them toward a logical decision when appropriate.

> Validation is not the same as agreeing with an idea or believing emotions need nurtured.

Valued

We each long to feel valued. God created us with a desire to appreciate others and feel appreciated. We want to be understood, which means those around us "get us." Our family sees our quirks and idiosyncrasies as part of who we are. They see our purpose in life, and they value our contributions to our family and to the world.

Just like us, the next generation wants to know that they are not a mistake, that they exist for a purpose, and that their dreams and ambitions matter. They need to understand they are priceless and precious. They look to parents, grandparents, caregivers, teachers, and other trusted adults to reinforce this desire to be valued. When they grasp their worth, they have a reason to live, to get out of bed each morning and interact with others. They're motivated to set goals and work toward them.

Help them visualize the future and set short-term and long-term goals. Give them chores and feasible tasks around the house, starting at a young age, so they feel appreciated and learn the value of contributing to the family. Encourage them in their likes and endeavors. Empower them to say no to peers who pressure them into behaviors that lead them away from their objectives. When they fail, acknowledge their setback and teach them how to recover. Be their cheerleader.

Our complex task is to see our children as special, seek to understand them, love them as they are, teach them how valuable they are, and point them to the One who will continue to love them, accept them, and show them their worth as they mature into adulthood. Whew! This job is strenuous and lengthy, but worth it. We are investing in our children.

No matter who we are, when our emotions act up, we're inclined to seek solace as fast as possible in whatever place is convenient. Awareness of these basic human needs allows us to be proactive in meeting them, both our own and those of our children. If we are aware that our anger, fear, anxiety, or need for love, acceptance, validation, or belonging is the source of an emotional outburst, we can override the emotions with logic and reasoning. We can return to what we know is true: God is love. Our love, acceptance, and validation come from him. Furthermore, if we have someone to turn to who will encourage us to work through emotions, we can use that resource, that healthy relationship, to supplement our needs.

But if the brain isn't fully developed and our emotions are out of control, we may look elsewhere for comfort. If we don't have a solid foundation and don't think others will help us, we may turn to someone or something outside ourselves (think food, alcohol, shopping, sex, pornography, etc.) to soothe our screaming emotions. These are distractions. That's how our children get mixed up with the wrong crowd, make poor choices, and end up in unhealthy online relationships. That's why they may send nudes and are vulnerable to sexual exploitation. Their needs aren't met, or they don't believe their needs are met.

When our children understand their worth, have a positive and safe environment at home, and are learning about God's love, they're less likely to turn to other people or things to meet their needs. When a new friend on social media asks about their day, they're less apt to confess their inner turmoil to her. When gaming with strangers, they're not as enticed by a request to meet up without telling anyone. Instead, they find healthy avenues to satisfy their inner desire to fit in.

Discern Needs

Someone who loves selflessly meets a loved one where they are without any expectations. She also pays attention, discerns the loved one's need, and then fulfills the need herself or guides the loved one toward the answer. Loving selflessly means looking past the obvious, past the presenting problem. It means searching for the underlying ache causing the turmoil.

I've learned that when my emotions take over—when I'm irritated, snippy, or exceptionally weepy—the inciting incident isn't necessarily the culprit. I'm not referring to the hormonal and chemical imbalance women experience because of their cycle (a real occurrence but not an excuse for uncalled-for behavior); I'm talking about emotions that indicate an unresolved issue that was initiated from an unmet need.

When I recognize these irrational behaviors invading my world and have sense enough to pause and take an honest appraisal, I usually trace my emotional outbursts back to feelings of inadequacy (not accepted), insecurity (not loved), loneliness (not belonging), worry or fear (not safe and secure), not being heard (not validated), or condemnation (not valued). If I don't pause, I'm liable to lash out in anger, run to food for comfort, wallow in self-pity, or any combination of these.

But when I identify the unfulfilled intrinsic longing, whether perceived or real, I'm able to sort through the issues and pinpoint the actual problem. Then I can work on a plan to resolve it. At times I talk it out with my husband. Sometimes I hash it out with God through prayer, Bible reading, and journaling. I may need to have an in-depth conversation with someone who is offending me, intentionally or unintentionally. Sometimes, through these moments, I realize I'm projecting my standards of conduct onto another. At that point, I attempt to drop those expectations.

It's taken me years to understand this cycle. Let's help our children make this connection. Let's sit with them when they are hurting, angry, or experiencing defeat. Ask questions, and remind them of our unconditional love. Let's help them feel safe and secure without squashing their dreams or ignoring their longings.

Check Motives

Being available to our children requires self-discipline and self-control. When we interact with them, we should check our motives. Are we receiving agape love from Christ and pouring out love from a place of wholeness? Or are we attempting to patch a problem because we want our lives to be carefree, comfortable, and untroubled? I ask myself these questions regularly. When my children interrupt my routine, are my actions motivated by an internal desire to return to my checklist or a selfless love to serve my offspring? How I respond to their requests may look the same either way, but they can sense the tension, the slight difference, if I don't have their best interest in mind.

Checking our own motives is tough enough. But we want to instill this skill in our children, particularly as they mature through puberty and college, when their hormones are in full swing, when they're physically attracted to others, and when they are more apt to get involved with online relationships or other toxic behaviors.

We want them to understand the difference between self-sacrificing love, lust, and infatuation. Both lust, based solely on physical attraction, and infatuation, a short-lived emotion, are selfish. These will wither away, whereas agape love will sustain the test of time.

Conversely, we want to distinguish the difference between selfless love and being a doormat. Girls are especially prone to believe that true love requires meeting a partner's needs no matter the cost to themselves. If they aren't aware of the distinctions, they may end up in an abusive relationship. Our job is to model true love and help the next generation understand healthy versus unhealthy behaviors so they search for someone who respects them and treats them well. It's not only about offering agape love but looking for someone who reciprocates that same type of love. We'll dive further into this concept in the next chapter.

Sex and Selflessness

When my son was sixteen, he attended a youth group meeting during which the male leader spoke with the guys about pornography and enumerated the ramifications porn could have on marriages and families. He learned that porn could seep into all areas of life and that many couples aren't able to withstand the damaging effects. The addiction drives wedges in relationships with spouses and trickles down to the children. Many marriages end in divorce.

The conversation was a turning point for him. He had been hiding his pornography use from us again, and one of the main reasons he felt convicted to seek our help was learning the devastating effects porn could have on his relationship with his girlfriend, presently or down the road. And he didn't want to ruin his future marriage by defiling it with pornography. He looked outside himself, realized his actions influenced others, and chose a selfless love for his eventual bride-to-be. I'm grateful his youth leader broached this awkward subject.

One area that doesn't get much attention when we talk about selflessness is sex. The church, in general, has done a poor job of teaching about sex. We've tiptoed and talked in hushed tones. We've ignored and pretended, hoping the subject matter will slip into the background and resolve itself. We've also been brash and bold, only to be scolded for being old-fashioned and out of touch.

But as Christians have flailed and failed, the issue has escalated, causing us to cower or act dumbfounded. We're simply afraid of getting it wrong—for good reason. Historically, we've botched it up, and it's easier to stick our heads in the sand than confront our own mess and start over. But we won't win this battle by feigning its existence. Society is more confused than ever, and the next generation deserves to know the truth. Let's be courageous enough to admit our shortcomings and try again.

The purity culture was in full swing when my older children were young. As they entered puberty and I had *the talk* with them, I also encouraged them to take a pledge or a vow of purity. I'm not saying this was inherently wrong, but the emphasis of purity culture centered on what not to do, rather than what to do.

In the article "Purity Culture and Its Unfortunate Intersection with Porn," Lisa Eldred, a content strategist at Covenant Eyes, explains that the education of purity culture on abstinence and modesty originated with positive motives but resulted in performance-based teachings. Rather than promoting a relationship with Jesus, purity culture taught teens to wonder how far was too far and whether dating or courting was the proper way to get to know a potential spouse. In the meantime, parents rarely talked about sex in a positive light, if at all.[1]

Through purity culture, Eldred continues, women learned it was their job to keep the visually stimulated opposite sex from lusting by wearing modest clothing and dictating how far was too far. Men believed they couldn't exercise self-control, and girls were burdened with a load too big to carry. And, after marriage, they weren't able to mentally switch from *sex is bad* to *sex is good*.

Eldred points out that as this movement was gaining ground, the Internet was introducing pornography to the world. Since parents didn't understand the importance of filters and monitoring screen time, teens—girls and boys alike—found their sexual outlet through watching porn. This, combined with the *wait until you're married or you're damaged goods* message of purity culture, led to secrecy, guilt, and shame.

When teens failed to keep the standards set for them within the purity culture, when they broke their vow of purity, they felt defeated. The church (and, truthfully, the parents who bought into this purity culture trend) failed to link sexual missteps with Christ's redemptive power. Understanding Christ's selfless love, the grace and mercy he extends, should be the motivation behind a pure life. We are pure because he makes us pure. We walk in obedience to his Word because he first loved us and we love him. And when we falter, we return to him, receive his grace and mercy, and become cleansed—purified—through his blood.[2]

When we talk about sex and sexuality with our children—yes, we must talk about it—let's start with Christ and his redemptive power. After all, marriage is to reflect the picture of Christ and his bride. We are cleansed and made whole through his blood. He is faithful to purify us and make us holy. Let's help our children grasp the freeing power of the gospel message so they willingly admit their wrongdoings to a loving God and seek his grace.

> When we talk about sex and sexuality with our children--yes, we must talk about it—let's start with Christ and his redemptive power.

We don't have to discuss the specifics of our sex lives, but we should paint a positive picture of sex. It's not taboo. It's not a sneaky, shameful behavior. We desire our children to enjoy sex and have positive sexual experiences—at the right time, under the right circumstances, with the right person.

Take an honest appraisal of your thoughts and feelings regarding sex. Some parents don't talk about sex and sexuality because they don't have a healthy view of it themselves. For years, I equated sex with love. I assumed if the sex between us was good, the relationship was good. While there is a connection, one does not equal the other.

I remember the first time I invited Christ into the bedroom. I realized God was all-knowing, all-seeing, and all-powerful, so he was there whether I acknowledged his presence or not. I opted to seek his guidance through the process. Before then, I kept my spiritual life separate from my intimate life, like it was a secret. When I prayed through my sexual experiences, I felt more relaxed and comfortable.

How do you view sex? Do you see it as a God-given gift? Do you believe it's a healthy expression of selfless love between a husband and wife? Is it for pleasure as well as for procreation? Consider the following verses. You may want to read them in context.

> Husbands, love your wives, just as Christ loved the church and gave himself up for her to make her holy, cleansing her by the washing with water through the word, and to present her to himself as a radiant church, without stain or wrinkle or any other blemish, but holy and blameless. In this same way, husbands ought to love their wives as their own bodies. He who loves his wife loves himself. After all, no one ever hated their own body, but they feed and care for their body, just as Christ does the church—for we are members of his body. "For

this reason a man will leave his father and mother and be united to his wife, and the two will become one flesh." This is a profound mystery—but I am talking about Christ and the church. However, each one of you also must love his wife as he loves himself, and the wife must respect her husband. (Eph. 5:25–33)

The husband should fulfill his marital duty to his wife, and likewise the wife to her husband. The wife does not have authority over her own body but yields it to her husband. In the same way, the husband does not have authority over his own body but yields it to his wife. Do not deprive each other except perhaps by mutual consent and for a time, so that you may devote yourselves to prayer. Then come together again so that Satan will not tempt you because of your lack of self-control. (1 Cor. 7:3–5)

May your fountain be blessed,
 and may you rejoice in the wife of your youth.
A loving doe, a graceful deer—
 may her breasts satisfy you always,
 may you ever be intoxicated with her love.
 (Prov. 5:18–19)

Song of Songs is also a good resource, as this book presents details of a lover and his beloved, demonstrating that sexual relations are enjoyable.

Once you've deciphered your views and perspective on sex, talk with your children. Remind them that sex is an important component of marriage and is intended to enhance a relationship and bond between a husband and wife. Our objective is to help them understand when sex is appropriate, teach them how to exercise self-control until marriage, and explain what selflessness looks like in the bedroom. Even within intimate relations, love "does not dishonor others, it is not self-seeking, it is not easily angered, it keeps no record of wrongs. Love does not delight in evil but rejoices with the truth" (1 Cor. 13:5–6).

Helping them understand selflessness within the context of agape love now sets them up to succeed in future relationships.

CHAPTER

5

Mutuality

The husband should fulfill his marital duty to his wife,
and likewise the wife to her husband. (1 Cor. 7:3)

When Don and I tied the knot, I was still trying to figure out this marriage business. The failure of my first marriage weighed heavily on me. I felt responsible: I was too forceful, too emotional, too unpredictable, too needy.

I began following Christ a few years into that first union. As my relationship with Christ grew, my demeanor changed slowly. As I leaned into God and started relying on him to fill my needs and guide my decisions, he refined my character. Still, confusion about the roles of a husband and wife lingered.

I entered my first marriage as a dominant personality, steering the direction of our lives. I didn't intend to take over; it just sort of happened. (At least, that's my perception.) The second time, I was determined to change. I believed (and still do) that the husband is the head of the household, but I remained puzzled as to the wife's role.

Shortly after saying our vows, I left my full-time job to be a stay-at-home homeschool mom of two little boys. I felt like I was living in a foreign land and impersonating an alien. Was I supposed to wear dresses and an apron, cook all day, and have an immaculate house? (Think June Cleaver, for those of you who remember the 1950s and 1960s show *Leave It to Beaver*.) Was I supposed to take all my cues from my husband and listen intently, nod passionately, and agree dutifully? That seemed extreme. But if I wasn't to control the marriage and wasn't to take a passive role, how was I to act? Where was the balance, the in-between, the sweet spot? It took me years to figure that out. The jobs and responsibilities are fluid, fluctuating as our circumstances change.

As life progresses, so do roles within marriages, but as the roles within marriages ebb and flow, mutual respect should remain constant. Neither person is more important than the other. Interactions, communication, and decisions ought to reflect this notion.

> As the roles within marriages ebb and flow, mutual respect should remain constant.

Why is this important to note? Analyzing our own thoughts and beliefs involving submission, respect, and each person's function within a marriage helps us teach our children how to thrive in a healthy relationship. Of course, no two marriages are identical, but understanding our core values is useful.

I struggled for years trying to find my place as a wife. I wrestled with Scripture, the ethics of society, and the teachings of the church. I'm grateful for those moments. I'm thankful that God—and my husband—provided space for me to ask questions, seek guidance, and flounder through the chaotic messages.

Consider your thoughts and beliefs regarding each person's role within a marriage. Can you offer a judgment-free zone to discuss these ideas with your children? Think about other relationships. What are the roles within friendships, sibling relationships, and work environments?

What Is Mutuality?

The messages in hookup culture, pornography, and online media imply a mutuality that doesn't actually exist. The underlying themes suggest those involved are taking charge of their lives, analyzing their choices, and selecting what's best for all participants. But in practicality, it's not panning out. In many hookups, one or both participants walk away dissatisfied sexually or emotionally, feeling used, or having been assaulted.

Pornography promotes physical and sexual assault, women as commodities, and racism by showing one race of men being aggressive toward a different race of women.[1] Online gaming promotes violence by portraying women as sex objects.[2] Partakers of either see idealistic body shapes and unrealistic sex acts and are conditioned to believe they should live up to these expectations. Certain people and groups on social media reinforce these ideas. This viewpoint is the opposite of the messages we want our children to learn.

Mutuality means sharing and supporting each other. Christlike love shows mutual respect, influence, and accountability. Each person encourages the other in their dreams, goals, and aspirations while being loyal, honest, and trustworthy. They do life together. Their love is reciprocal. It's important for us to define mutuality and direct the next generation to healthier interactions and attitudes concerning partnerships, friendships, and marriage.

Let's look at part of the 1 Corinthians passage again.

> Love is patient, love is kind. It does not envy, it does not boast, it is not proud. It does not dishonor others, it is not self-seeking, it is not easily angered, it keeps no record of wrongs. Love does not delight in evil but rejoices with the truth. It always protects, always trusts, always hopes, always perseveres. (1 Cor. 13:4–7)

In healthy relationships, all these aspects of love intertwine, but let's probe a few of them. We'll unpack patience and kindness in the chapter on communication. We discussed selflessness, or "not self-seeking," in the previous chapter. Certainly, mutuality goes hand in hand with these, but the portion of the 1 Corinthians passage that speaks directly to mutuality is, "It does not dishonor . . . It always protects, always trusts, always hopes, always perseveres." We honor everyone because God created all in the image of Christ. We honor those in close relationships by considering their ideas, emotions, and ambitions. Protect their reputation. Trust and be trustworthy.

People in a healthy relationship hope and persevere, and they don't give up at the first sign of trouble, trauma, or heartbreak. Persevering, however, doesn't mean holding onto a relationship no matter what. There are limitations. After all, we're still imperfect people. While love always perseveres, a loving action may be to step away from an unhealthy relationship. Please don't hear me say that someone in a toxic or abusive marriage must, or must not, pursue a divorce—that's a subject I can't speak to within the confines of this book.

> People in a healthy relationship hope and persevere, and they don't give up at the first sign of trouble, trauma, or heartbreak.

When parents, grandparents, and caregivers can distinguish the difference between healthy and unhealthy relationships, they can pass the information along to those in their care. Ideally, the next generation *only* enters healthy relationships. However, that goal is far-fetched. The next-best option is helping them recognize signs of unhealthy relationships, ones that don't offer mutuality, so they can leave before they're in too deep. The earlier someone notices these signals, the quicker they can remove themselves from the situation. Walking away from a long-term relationship or marriage is more difficult and problematic than breaking up the moment they discern something is amiss. The trick is spotting the dishonorable behavior.

Red Flags

A friend of mine, a married woman, didn't realize she was in an abusive marriage because she grew up in a home where abuse was rampant. She thought pushing and shoving were acceptable because they weren't full-on slaps or punches to the face. Likewise, another believed name-calling was okay because her husband wasn't physically assaulting her. Later, these ladies learned these actions weren't appropriate and the relationships were unhealthy. Even if no one in a relationship is aggressive, we can understand how the lines between healthy and unhealthy can be puzzling and how our children can be confused given the conduct promoted in mainstream TV shows, movies, music, and games.

How can we tell if a relationship is unhealthy, toxic, or abusive? The younger generation is familiar with the terms *red flags* and *green flags*. They even use emoji shortcuts to signify red and green flags. Below are listed some red flags, some unhealthy indicators. We mostly spot these in dating or marriage relationships, but they can also be seen in friendships, work environments, and family dynamics.

The other person:

- Shows regular signs of jealousy
- Tries to isolate you; tells you not to talk to or mingle with anyone, even your parents or siblings
- Is easily angered
- Lies
- Calls you names, puts you down, or won't listen to you
- Never apologizes; always blames you for their behaviors and problems in the relationship
- Doesn't respect your boundaries
- Is controlling; makes all the decisions and manipulates you and your responses
- Has an addiction they aren't willing to address
- Abuses you physically or verbally

When you are around this person, you feel:

- Embarrassed
- Intimidated
- Guilty
- Inadequate

- ▶ Incompetent
- ▶ Hurt
- ▶ Stupid
- ▶ Devalued
- ▶ Manipulated
- ▶ Pressured
- ▶ Unsafe, physically and/or emotionally
- ▶ Trapped
- ▶ Nervous
- ▶ Depressed
- ▶ Desperate for their attention, love, or approval
- ▶ Inauthentic, as if you need to be someone you're not

In addition to detecting any of the above signals, when someone you trust—a parent, sibling, teacher, coach, counselor, pastor, or friend—tells you she sees red flags, take a step back and observe the relationship from an outsider's perspective. Maybe there are behaviors you haven't noticed.

Trust your gut. If you sense a problem, explore it. Even if you're insecure because of issues in past relationships, it's worth taking a break from the current situation to allow space for healing.

Everyone has a right to be treated with kindness and respect. Matthew 7:12 says, "So in everything, do to others what you would have them do to you." Offer grace and allow for imperfection, but if you see consistent red-flag behavior without a willingness by the other person to address the issues, it may be time to walk away.

Green Flags

How can we discern if a relationship is healthy?

Here are some green flags that signal the relationship is strong and healthy.

The other person:

- Trusts you
- Encourages you to have other relationships—with friends, coworkers, and family
- Values your thoughts; listens when you express opinions or emotions
- Treats you with kindness and gentleness
- Respects you and your boundaries
- Points you toward Christ and biblical principles
- Allows space within the relationship for discussions and differing perspectives
- Keeps their word; follows through on promises
- Admits wrongdoing; sees faults and apologizes when appropriate
- Encourages you to pursue your goals and dreams
- Celebrates your successes

When you are around this person, you feel:

- Loved
- Honored
- Respected
- Comfortable
- Competent
- Valued
- Validated
- Safe
- Secure

► Content
► Authentic; able to be your true self

In healthy relationships, both parties experience green-flag actions and feelings. The connection includes give and take, back and forth, reciprocity—and the motive is genuine agape love for each other.

Love Languages Defined

When we love someone, we want to express it. But how do we determine how *they* like to be loved? I can think of no better way to discover how to love than to delve into Gary Chapman's well-known love languages. Chapman first wrote *The 5 Love Languages* in 1992 and has released multiple revisions and supplemental books on the subject since.[3] But the love languages remain the same.

Words of Affirmation

Most people appreciate their efforts being acknowledged, but some of us feel loved best when others affirm us with their words.

When Don and I first married, I worked full-time. My boss thanked me for my hard work verbally, through notes, and with small gifts. We'll get to gifts in a moment, but I didn't feel valued because of the mint ice cream sundaes from Dairy Queen (my favorite!) or the florist-delivered flowers (those gave me sinus infections). I felt appreciated because my boss noticed my hard work and expressed his gratitude.

When I quit my job a few months into our marriage, I worried about staying home all day with two four-year-olds and no adult to ~~help me keep my sanity~~ acknowledge my efforts. I told Don about my apprehension and asked him to recognize me and the work I accomplished all day. He listened. When the kids were young, I homeschooled and completed all the housework. He thanked me for specific tasks, like teaching the children or cooking meals. He also reminded me that my skills and character traits were appreciated, which bolstered my resolve to strive for excellence. To this day, he often compliments me and tells me he's grateful I'm his wife. He reassures me by telling me how proud he is of me. His words of affirmation are especially uplifting on days I feel unproductive or useless.

Showing Don love is easy since his primary love language, like mine, is words of affirmation, but I still need to be intentional. One of my favorite ways to express my love to him is by talking about his accomplishments to others when he's within earshot. I also make a point of complimenting him on social media—a public space.

People who experience love through words of affirmation can be sensitive regarding hurtful words or lack of communication. They are more apt to sense rejection or underappreciation if their efforts go unnoticed. Preteens and teens whose primary love language is words of affirmation may fall prey to online connections, even with strangers, who compliment (flatter) them often. These actions may be used to lure them into toxic relationships.

If you have a spouse, children, or friends who use this love language, actively listen when they speak, and sincerely compliment them often.

Quality Time
People whose primary love language is quality time feel loved best when others spend time with them and give them undivided attention. Sitting on the couch together watching a movie may count,

but typically, quality-time people prefer an interactive activity. Grab lunch. Play a game. Go for a bike ride. Do the dishes together. Learn what they enjoy, and schedule a time for it.

While words of affirmation is my primary love language, quality time is my secondary. I feel loved when my husband takes a walk with me or spends the day at the beach with me. One of my favorite activities is playing games with my family. My heart fills when we sit around the dining room table and play a board game together. Inevitably, one of the more animated family members tells a joke, which leads to another. Soon enough, I'm laughing so hard I can't quit.

People with this love language may feel unloved if you don't schedule regular time together. Children with this love language may fall prey to online connections, even strangers, who spend time listening and understanding their dilemmas. They may tolerate abusive behavior because any interaction is better than none.

When relating to these loved ones, give them your full attention. Don't wait for them to initiate an activity. Be proactive. Put away distractions, including your phone.

Receiving Gifts

People with this love language feel loved best when someone gives them a gift, big or small, expensive or inexpensive. Because we typically express love the way we like to be loved, we can easily spot a person with this love language: toddlers who pick flowers for their mom; preschoolers who make cards for their parents, grandparents, aunts, friends, and next-door neighbors; a husband who surprises his wife with unexpected gifts or whisks her away on a getaway at a moment's notice; a friend who shows up for a coffee date with a wrapped package.

I learned late in life this was a thing. I don't like surprises, and I'm not one for relentless small tokens of affection. It took me several years to discover that one of my children possesses this love language. I missed many opportunities to show my love to him while he was growing up, often saying no to purchases I deemed unwarranted. Thankfully, I eventually detected it and now arrive with a gift in hand when I visit him. Sometimes, it's just one of his favorite snacks.

The upside for the gift giver is that the recipient treasures anything you give them. Of course, they may also feel unloved if you miss a birthday or don't recognize their desire. Children with this love language may be lured into an unhealthy relationship, online or in person, by gifts. If you see your preteen or teen with new things, ask where the items came from.

When interacting with these loved ones, remember to give them gifts, even small ones, often.

Acts of Service

Those with this love language appreciate help with their day-to-day responsibilities. The way to express love to people with an acts-of-service love language is by coming alongside them while they are accomplishing a task, be it cleaning the bathroom, grocery shopping, or cooking supper, with a cheerful attitude and without being asked. Help lighten the load of their list of duties.

If you offer to help, be sure to follow through. Someone with this love language will feel rejected if you promise to schedule an appointment for them, pick up bread while you're out, or unload the dishwasher, and you forget. They feel unloved if their expectations go unmet. Children with this love language may fall into an unhealthy relationship when an outsider offers to help with their responsibilities or criticizes an authority figure's lack of care for the child.

When interacting with loved ones who possess this love language, quietly start drying the dishes while they are washing them, make their bed before they have a chance, or ask them how you can help them. If you sense they're overwhelmed or they brush you off, offer options and ask which would be most helpful. Observe their routine, and jump in when you can.

Physical Touch

People with this love language feel loved best when they are touched. In this case, physical touch is referring to non-sensual touch. This person may like to sit close, hug, or hold hands.

My youngest son's love language is physical touch. When he was little, he leaned on me while I cooked or cleaned the dishes. He was always close. He sat right next to me or climbed all over me. He poked me and grabbed my face. I felt like he was suffocating me, as he was in my personal space all the time. It drove me nuts.

When I take quizzes on love languages, I score low on this one. My pulse races when people are close to me for an extreme amount of time. (My definition of extreme is anything over three minutes.) My son's constant need for physical touch was exhausting.

My daughter's love language is also physical touch. When we first met, she'd run to me and give me big hugs or kiss my face. She enjoyed cuddling and holding hands. After she came home, it was clear that she and her brother could fulfill each other's need for love. They bonded immediately by wrestling, climbing together, or sitting close. Even now, as adults, they still put their arms around each other or link arms. When my son is home from college, I frequently see him sneak up on his sister and give her a bear hug, put her in a headlock, or sit on top of her. She's a great sport and receives it as an expression of love.

Those with this love language feel unloved or rejected when physically neglected. Children with this love language may be more susceptible to unhealthy partners who use physical touch to manipulate them into a toxic relationship.

If you have children with this love language, remember to touch them in appropriate ways frequently. A quick shoulder rub, playing with their hair, or a light touch on the arm goes a long way.

Love Languages and Mutuality

Expressions of love can cross over love languages. For example, my sister gives exceptional gifts. She spends a great deal of time selecting unique presents, personalized to each receiver. When she mails me a gift, I feel loved because the item says "I see you" (words of affirmation) and "I did something special for you" (acts of service), not just "here's a gift." When someone offers me a hug, in my eyes they are extending quality time as well as physical touch. Which brings me to another point: there are exceptions. Even though I score low on physical touch, I enjoy giving hugs. (I'm squeamish about handshakes, though, as I'm pretty weird about keeping my hands clean.)

We typically show love the way we feel loved. But if a husband's love language is gifts and his wife expresses her love to him by helping with the lawn and other acts of service, he may not notice—her interference may even irritate him. If she never shows him love through his love language—gifts—he may feel unloved, and a problem in their relationship may develop. Our default is to express love how we receive it, but agape love pursues another through their love language.

> Our default is to express love how we receive it, but agape love pursues another through their love language.

After I learned the five love languages, I had a revelation. I understood why I felt more loved by some people than others *and* why I felt more rejected by some. This tool also clarified some of my children's behaviors and signs of love.

When we aren't meeting our children's needs for love at home, or they don't perceive our love for them, they're more apt to fall prey to an online predator or seek fulfillment in hookups or otherwise unhealthy outlets.

We each have a primary and secondary love language. After reviewing the five love languages, are you able to identify your primary and secondary? Can you pinpoint your children's? Do you see your spouse's? Parents'? Friends'? Do you understand the benefits of discovering them?

Explain your love language to your family members, and help them define theirs. A fun exercise may be for each person to list three to five ways the others can express love to them.

Reciprocal Trust

"Why did you move the juice from the drink shelf to the door?" I fired this question at my husband one morning.

"I don't know."

Was that a defensive tone I heard? "Hmpf."

Silence ensued, but my irritation was evident, and my suspicions were mounting. By lunch, I was convinced Don was on a personal mission to ruin my life by rearranging all the food in the refrigerator, one object at a time. He knew I organized the food a particular way and preferred all the drinks on the third shelf. When I opened the fridge at lunch, my hunch was confirmed. The lettuce was in the wrong drawer. The last straw? Broken.

I launched an attack. "You know how I like the food arranged. You know it frustrates me when I can't find things. You moved the juice and the lettuce on purpose just to upset me."

Don stood there with his mouth open. "I don't know what you're talking about."

I had to admit, he looked confused. "Oh." I walked away.

This wasn't the first time I had accused him of some outlandish ruse against me. Upon further reflection, I remembered times I'd been defensive when he asked me a question. I tended to look for hidden meaning, the *real* motive, behind each query.

These crazy scenarios concocted in my head were manifestations of insecurity. I didn't believe Don's love for me was unwavering. I didn't trust his motives, and I didn't think he trusted mine.

When my rational self appeared, I apologized to Don. We admitted we each leaned toward skepticism and resolved to assume the other's motives were pure and loving, even when our actions or words didn't read as such. That means I pause when I feel myself getting agitated over something Don did. I ask myself if the question I'm about to spout is important and check my motive for asking it. Before proceeding, I examine my vocal tone and body language. Then I phrase the question in a manner that won't cause Don to automatically become defensive.

Love trusts. Love believes the best. When we believe our loved one, spouse, parent, child, or friend has pure motives, we are less defensive and more forgiving. We're open to their suggestions. The atmosphere within the relationship is relaxing and allows for pleasant exchanges. We feel comfortable talking about our heart-aches and our dreams, our hurts and our limitations. We express our boundaries without fear of judgment or retribution.

Boundaries

I ruffled my son's hair. "Good job." He had finished his science project and was walking it to the living room to show his dad.

"You messed up my hair." He appeared less than thrilled.

"But it's so soft," I said playfully.

"Mom, stop. I don't like when you get in my space."

I paused. I guess he was growing up and no longer appreciated his mommy touching him without permission. "Sorry. I'll try to be more respectful."

I can't boast that I've always heard my children's requests or taken them seriously. I also can't promise I never ruffled my son's hair again—I may have slipped once or twice. But as I mature, I'm learning to listen to others when they attempt to communicate their boundaries.

When teaching preteens and teens at local schools, we empha-size the importance of setting and communicating boundaries. A healthy person institutes boundaries. Healthy relationships incor-porate boundaries. A boundary is a limit. It's a border, an invisible line drawn to express parameters—what we deem as acceptable and unacceptable in various areas of life. Think of a fence or lines on a road. The lines mark the area where it's safe to drive. If we veer over the line, we're in danger of hitting an oncoming car or going into a ditch.

I like boundaries. I find them comforting. Not everyone appreciates limitations and rules, but I feel safer knowing them and staying within their confines. I'd much rather my son tell me not to touch his hair, even though this signal that he was growing up saddened me, than for him to resent me because I crossed a boundary I didn't know existed.

Our goal as caregivers is to help our children (1) comprehend why they need boundaries, (2) recognize which areas of life need boundaries, (3) set their boundaries, and (4) communicate their boundaries to others.

Boundaries protect us. Many people rebel against rules and regulations. Society conditions us to resist guidelines and directives, as if those "other people" are trying to control, manipulate, and reign over us. Hormonal teens, trying to find their place in the world and testing their limits, can adopt this stance. Our objective is to turn this thinking around so they view boundaries as friendly and an essential component of life.

When I tell teens we turn off the Wi-Fi every night at 11:00 p.m. in our household, they look at me as if I've lost my mind and ruined my children for life. But I purposefully mention this limit to reveal this fact: because I love my children, I want to safeguard them. My job is to protect them from predators and help them resist temptation late at night. I am relieving them of the burden of saying no to pornography, late-night gaming, and social media drama—and improving their ability to say yes to a good night's sleep and a well-rested body.

Boundaries are necessary in multiple areas of life. We set our alarms. We create budgets. We watch our caloric intake. We limit our interactions with people who push our buttons. And we obey traffic signals. These are all boundaries—ones we've set for ourselves and ones established by others. To some extent, these lines exist in all areas of life, but let's look at some specific areas that benefit relationships. We want the next generation to set these boundaries as soon as possible, before it's necessary to exercise them.

In the physical area, within a romantic relationship, help your children establish how far they will go sexually before marriage. Discuss the options, lay out the benefits of waiting for intercourse, read Scripture, and pray with them. Walk them through the stages of physical intimacy, including holding hands, kissing, and other sexual activity leading up to intercourse, being as explicit as possible for their age. Help them choose their line, their stopping point, but allow them to make the choice. When comfortable, tell personal stories—your choices and the benefits and/or consequences of your decisions. Offer advice if they ask, but don't decide for them. Preteens and teens are more apt to adhere to limits, to say no when pressured, if they set their boundaries themselves.

Determine boundaries around screen time and social media. Get their buy-in by asking for their input and listening to their reasoning. Ask their opinion about consequences when needed. The parameters established in your home depend on your children's ages, maturity level, and history. Some children are more vulnerable than others. Some have a more addictive nature than others. As they mature, adapt the guidelines. Hopefully, as adults, they will continue to place limits on their screen time.

Additionally, help your children decipher acceptable and unacceptable behaviors within friendships, partnerships, and family. Do your children like teasing? How close is too close? Do others listen to their ideas? Do they have the freedom to make decisions within relationships, or do others always demand their way? Are they confident enough to interact with other people responsibly? Do they encounter abusive behavior? Are they treated with respect and kindness? Do others pressure them when they say no? Are they looking for red flags?

Do your children know when someone crosses a line? How will they respond?

We want the next generation to regard these borders as positive and protective so, as they mature into adulthood, they continue to set them and say no to people who push for more.

After they've determined their boundaries, help your children communicate those boundaries. We'll talk more in-depth about communication in the next chapter, but I want to emphasize here that voicing boundaries is important. The sooner we empower our children to set and communicate boundaries, the better equipped they will be for the future. Teach them to state their limitations in a kind manner and say "no" when the lines are ignored. If someone continuously pushes their limits, they may need to change the approach to the relationship.

> The sooner we empower our children to set and communicate boundaries, the better equipped they will be for the future.

It's reasonable to set our own boundaries and adhere to others' limits. Acknowledging and appreciating others' boundaries is important. This give-and-take contributes to a healthy, mutually respectful relationship.

Relationship Rhythm

"When's the last time you went out with your friends?" Don asked me this question over coffee.

"I don't know." I couldn't remember the last time I'd left the house without one of my kids. Sure, we attended church, and I visited the grocery store and library once a week. But when had I spent time alone with a friend?

I'd awakened that morning feeling depressed. My life consisted of homeschooling our children, making three meals a day, and taking care of our home. I loved my husband and my children, but my routine was monotonous. My husband could sense my restlessness.

"Have you been exercising?" he asked.

"No." The winter weather was dismal, and I couldn't talk myself into stepping onto the treadmill, which was located in our dark basement.

"Why don't you contact Suzie and see if you two can go to dinner tonight?" he suggested.

"It's too expensive." Our small budget had little margin. But something bigger than our finances stopped me. I feared Suzie would reject my suggestion—that she wouldn't want to spend time with me. For days, my thoughts had centered on my deficiencies as a parent, wife, and friend. It seemed like I fell short of everyone's expectations. Furthermore, I *wanted* to feel fulfilled in my role as wife and homeschool mom, but I *didn't*. I considered myself a fraud.

Thankfully, Don wasn't dismissive or uncaring. He was compassionate and accommodating. He listened to my dilemma and walked me through my options.

At the time, I knew the answer, at least temporarily, was to continue walking the path God already laid out for me while caring for myself. Self-care included outings with other moms, friends I relied on the first decade I homeschooled. My husband understood that need.

As my children grew and, one by one, left our home, my role changed. He supported me as I volunteered at churches, wrote, and worked part-time jobs. He thanked me for my contribution to our family and reminded me of my value.

Over the years, we've developed a rhythm. We've had each other's backs through five moves and numerous job changes. We've discussed ways to resolve conflicts with family and children. We've clung to each other through emergency room visits and chronic back pain. We've entertained each other on bad days. And we've often packed our bags and headed out of town for a brief respite to cut through the boredom, dreariness, or, more often, anxiety.

We encourage and support each other. We understand each other well enough to notice when the other is emotionally distressed or physically ill. We check in and ask questions, reminding each other we're available to talk, listen, or pray. When we see signs of unforgiveness, anger, or unacceptable behaviors, we advise each other. We push each other to reach goals and celebrate small successes. Neither of us feels inferior or superior to the other. Our unconditional love is mutual.

God First

A love that "does not dishonor" and "always protects, always trusts, always hopes, always perseveres" prioritizes the relationship above the individual. Neither person is more important. Neither is in control. Both recognize God as the one on the throne of the relationship. God rules and reigns circumstances and interactions. When each person bows to God's sovereignty, they are free to elevate each other, knowing that posture doesn't diminish either person's worth or position within the relationship.

> When each person bows to God's sovereignty, they are free to elevate each other, knowing that posture doesn't diminish either person's worth or position within the relationship.

Rather than feeling restrained, when we release control to God, which is merely acknowledging his authority, we are liberated. When each person allows God to reign, both are comfortable being themselves. Both protect the other and the relationship by being the other's advocate and biggest fan. Both cheer for the other. Both encourage the other to pursue their dreams and goals. Both hold the other close, but not to the point of suffocation. Both get in the trenches with the other, walking with them, pulling them out when possible, and pointing them to Christ. Both trust the other's motives and defend the other even when the behaviors aren't admirable. And each feels reassured and supported—loved.

When we're in a long-term relationship, when we've made a commitment to a friend, child, or spouse, we have a choice. We can simply tolerate them, allowing the uncertainties, issues, and idiosyncrasies to sway our thoughts and decisions. Or we can be all in, loving the other through the lens of Christ, focusing on their positive traits and characteristics. A long-term commitment requires determination and endurance. Relationships built on Christlike love, with selflessness and mutuality as important goals, will stand the test of time.

CHAPTER
6

Communication

The words of the reckless pierce like swords, but the tongue of the wise brings healing. (Prov. 12:18)

"Stop screaming!"

My toddler, strapped in his high chair, was attempting to tell me something. Unfortunately, I didn't know how to interpret this particular shriek.

I was serving lunch to my older children, and my youngest son's serenading screeches weren't setting the tone for a peaceful meal.

"Do you want more?" I held out a piece of banana. He grabbed for it. In an attempt to rid my house of the background noise, I acted on advice from a friend. "Say please," I said while rubbing my upper chest—sign language for the word *please*.

He stared at me. "Sss."

"Well, that works." I smiled and handed him the banana. We proceeded to eat in a quieter atmosphere.

He never learned the sign for *please*, but he could ask for more food without screaming. This is the same child who learned to put both hands in the air—his sign for "all done"—when he finished eating. This signal worked great until our summer vacation. On the first day, half an hour into the three-day cross-country trip, he threw his hands up in the air. He was "all done" sitting in his car seat. That first day was a doozy.

Communication Fluctuations

We send and receive messages all day: a look, a sound, a gesture, the way we walk, the way we pause mid-sentence, the way our voices rise and fall, a text, a post, a note, laughing, crying, smiling, frowning. These are all messages. Whether intentional or unintentional, whether perceived or real, we transmit ideas and opinions throughout the day to those in our vicinity.

We are created to connect, and connection requires communication. When we share our messages in a respectful and loving manner, we're more apt to enjoy healthy relationships. Just like the first three habits discussed in the previous chapters, we should refine this trait in our own lives, model it, and help our children convey their thoughts well.

There are different methods of interacting, and some children, like adults, are better at communicating than others. Our youngest son learned to speak early in life—after "sss" he never stopped talking. But I have children who weren't as chatty. Two pouted and shut down rather than using words. While in the process of adopting, Don and I visited our daughter in Guatemala. She was four years old and only spoke Spanish. One evening, we left our hotel room to walk to her favorite restaurant. We stopped at a store along the way. After two minutes of shopping, she plopped herself on the sidewalk, crossed her arms, stuck her lip out, and refused to look at me. I didn't need to know the Spanish words for *unhappy*, *mad*, or *stubborn* to comprehend her meaning. She received our message pretty clearly, too, when Don picked her up and carried her back to the hotel room. We ate in that night.

We think communication becomes easier as they mature, and it may, for a while. I liked when my kids were in the fourth and fifth grades. They were old enough to hold an intelligent conversation, and they still believed I was knowledgeable and trustworthy.

When the teen years hit, some mysteriously morph into beings who only use one-syllable words and sounds.

"Good morning."

"Hmmp."

"How was your day?"

"Fine."

"Will you be home for supper?"

"Uh-huh."

"Did you do anything exciting today?"

A look of contempt mixed with annoyance.

Some children vanish during their teen years. They lock themselves in their rooms, work, or hang out with friends, only appearing at mealtimes. When faced with a hormonal teen who shows no desire to interact with her parents, discerning when to let go and when to push is challenging. Add in stepchildren and extra parents in the form of ex-spouses, and learning how to communicate becomes more difficult.

> When faced with a hormonal teen who shows no
> desire to interact with her parents, discerning when
> to let go and when to push is challenging.

Not all children cease to talk when they hit age twelve, though. And not all of them believe their parents are clueless. A few of mine continued to treat us as if we had a few brain cells in our heads.

As parents, employing Christlike love may be more difficult as our children pull away and exercise their independence. However, when we cling to Christ and God's Word, recognize our child's love language, choose to love selflessly, and treat our children with mutuality, communicating is less complicated.

Signals

We constantly send signals.

When I was in high school, I was shy and insecure. I walked from class to class with my head down and greeted few people because I didn't think anyone knew me or wanted to interact with me. Later, I found out that my classmates interpreted my lack of acknowledgement as snobbish. They thought I was stuck-up. This conclusion was the opposite of the truth. I sent a signal—one that was misinterpreted, but a signal nonetheless.

Silence is a type of communication that's often misunderstood. Someone may choose to stay quiet during a meeting because she's shy, while another may be silent because she's angry. One may be lost in thought about an upcoming vacation, and another may be mulling over a fight last night with her spouse. Children refuse to communicate because they don't know how to express their feelings, they're overwhelmed, they're afraid of rejection, or they desire revenge. For years, I didn't tell my husband what I wanted because I assumed it was his job to read my mind. That didn't work out well.

When my husband doesn't answer me, I'm left rifling through the possibilities of his muteness. Is he ignoring me? Is he angry at me? Did he misunderstand my question? Is he thinking of an answer? Did he even hear me? Years ago, I allowed his silence to bother me. I felt hurt and rejected. I took it personally and reacted with accusations of insensitivity. But I've learned that if he doesn't respond to me within a minute or two, he most likely didn't hear me or doesn't think my comment requires a response.

If we aren't careful, we'll react to our children's silence. Whether or not they are purposefully ignoring us, we can respond in a loving, patient, gentle manner. If we react from a place of hurt, inadequacy, or frustration, we risk them stonewalling or resisting us.

Let's return to 1 Corinthians 13 and read what God says about love and how it intersects with communication.

> Love is patient, love is kind. It does not envy, it does
> not boast, it is not proud. It does not dishonor others,
> it is not self-seeking, it is not easily angered, it keeps
> no record of wrongs. Love does not delight in evil but
> rejoices with the truth. It always protects, always trusts,
> always hopes, always perseveres. (1 Cor. 13:4–7)

The culmination of loving someone—*expressing* our love to them— is through communication. In that sense, the above passage from 1 Corinthians is all about communicating. But the portion that best fits this habit is, "Love is patient, love is kind." Certainly, some people require more patience and kindness than others. Typically, those living in our homes are the ones who ~~get on our nerves~~ try our patience the most. And when our children hit those teen years and begin to roll their eyes, turn their backs, and look at us with disdain? Well, leaning into the Holy Spirit and crying out for his patience and kindness to flow through us become more important.

Blunders

Lest you think I have it all together and parented perfectly with patience and kindness flowing freely, permit me to list some communication mistakes I made with my children along the way. Then we'll evaluate how to remedy these blunders.

Being Dismissive

As a young mother, I wasn't tolerant of differing personalities and communication methods. In my attempt to control my environment, I put all objects, ideas, and people in figurative boxes. As you may have guessed, people, even little people, don't like to be categorized and pushed into molds, so they didn't always conform to my definition of proper behavior. When my children interrupted me, misunderstood my directives, or tried to express themselves using long paragraphs or garbled messages, I was impatient and exercised my authority by hushing them or dismissing them. I didn't listen well. I didn't value their thoughts and opinions. Their lack of understanding or confusing body language led to an emotional response that overpowered my job as a parent.

It is acceptable, at times, to remind our children to be quiet or to redirect them, but we want to check our motives before taking these actions. Do we have their best interest in mind? Are we teaching them proper social skills? Or are we attempting to make our environment more comfortable?

Talking at Them instead of with Them

I'm a teacher by nature—a great trait for a homeschool mom. What I didn't catch on to early enough is that certain personality types don't respond well to being told what to do all day long. Even those who welcome rules and instruction prefer dialogue over lecture. I assumed my children trusted me, believed God's Word to be true, and would automatically adhere to my advice without explanation or reasoning. However, if we don't allow space for them to ask questions or interpret facts and statistics on their own, they won't come to us when they question their beliefs or struggle with an issue.

Misinterpreting Their Signals

As I've stated, we communicate all day long. Sometimes, a breakdown occurs between the sender and the receiver. My children gave me the cold shoulder, goofed off, fidgeted, bickered, talked back, stared blankly, and shot me looks full of hatred. They laughed, cried, screamed, and gave me the silent treatment. They said one thing when they meant another. They hugged and kissed one day, and they held me at arm's length the next. In other words, they were normal. But as a young mother, I didn't always interpret their body language, silence, tears, words of anger, or mental collapses properly. Sometimes I saw temper tantrums rather than cries for help. I saw procrastination rather than a loss on how to proceed. In my zeal to shape their behavior, I periodically forgot to shape their person.

We all need people willing to look deep inside us, understand the message we're *trying* to send, and value who we are at our core.

Underestimating the Value of My Signals

I love deeply, but I don't always show it. Because of my high expectations, sometimes my children sensed they failed me.

My son felt salty because I never gave him a 100 percent on any papers he wrote for me. The day he received his first one hundred for a research paper he wrote in college, he told me, "I didn't know that was possible." We laugh about it now, but each of my children had real hurts because they interpreted my high standards as judgment and rejection.

We can't overestimate open demonstrations of unconditional love, especially through positive reinforcement.

Assuming One Talk Was Enough

This misstep applies to numerous topics, but the biggest is sex and sexuality. I failed to incorporate regular discussions about this vital issue into our everyday activities. I was conditioned through my upbringing and societal norms to believe parents wait until a certain age before opening the door to this subject. Then, they crack it open, peek inside, discuss what's behind the door as quickly as possible, and shut the door again. Afterward, everyone tiptoes around the shut door, pretending it doesn't exist.

When I explained the birds and the bees (*Why do we call it that?*) to my older boys, I read them a book. I asked Don to sit with us. I opened the book, lifted it high enough to cover my face, read straight through, snapped the book shut, and told my boys to see their dad if they had questions. The incident was awkward for everybody. Although we revisited the topic here and there, the one-way dialogues stemmed from concerning incidents and comprised me reminding them how to or not to behave. My reasoning was, "The Bible says . . ."

After my son's pornography issue surfaced, I realized the way parents address this issue needed to change.

> After my son's pornography issue surfaced, I realized the way parents address this issue needed to change.

Tips for Communicating Better

How do we interact with our children to foster a loving, trusting, relaxed environment? How do we model kindness and patience? How do we communicate our beliefs and instructions without alienating our children? How do we draw them near rather than push them away? How do we prioritize the relationship over transmitting information and changing behavior?

One myth we need to dispel is that communicating with our children, or anyone for that matter, transpires naturally. We're under the impression that the ability to interact with others easily is something we're born with, and if this knack is not innate, we're defective.

Communicating for the purpose of cultivating a healthy relationship is a learned behavior for many of us. If we want our children to truly believe we're available for them, to share their joys and sorrows, to listen or offer advice, to do life with, we should evaluate the pros and cons of how we currently communicate and adjust accordingly. Positive, healthy discussions require determination and practice.

This habit of healthy relationships, *communication*—whether verbal or nonverbal, oral or written, sending or receiving—is the point where all the habits meet. Our loved ones will believe we agape love them based on how we transmit our messages and interpret theirs.

Here are a few tips I've learned along the way:

Lift Your Head

Get your nose out of your phone and turn off your devices. Ouch! This one hurts. We've long been telling our children to put their devices down, but how often do we heed our own advice?

We had a "no phones at the table" policy in our household. For years we stuck to this rule, but as society adjusted, so did we. Now it's commonplace and acceptable to scroll while talking. Just last night my daughter asked a question while we were eating. I picked up my phone to search for an answer. When I looked up, all three of us had a phone in one hand and a fork in the other.

True connection requires active participation. Put the device away. Lean forward. Look the other person in the eyes. Nod. Shake your head. Respond when asked a question. Smile. Frown. Do the thing your emoji would show you were doing if the conversation were a text. Don't merely act interested; be interested. Care. People are fascinating. Pay attention and discover what's going on in their lives.

Listen. Listen. Listen.

Learn when to be silent and only listen.

This one is hard for me. I'm an interrupter. You know, the person who doesn't let you finish a sentence. But I'm learning I don't need to voice every thought that comes to mind, and I don't need to be "right" all the time. The relationship supersedes the necessity to win or express my opinion.

I don't need to fill silent moments with words. When I allow space for my children, husband, friends, etc., to think, to pause and wait, to be comfortable in the silence, they expose their innermost thoughts. We get to the root of the matter, and they feel heard.

Be Aware of Body Language

A high percentage of messages are communicated through body language. We lean in when we're engaged. We back up when we're disinterested or afraid. We tower over someone to show power and lower ourselves to show equality. Toddlers poke their parents to get their attention. Teens bat their eyes or flip their hair to flirt. They strut their stuff in confidence or slouch and hang their heads when feeling unnoticed, insecure, or ashamed.

My face is easy to read. Friends and family discern my thoughts and feelings through my animated expressions. There's no disguising my opposing opinion on an issue. My mouth turns inward. I squint my eyes. I take a deep breath. Those around me also detect my excitement. My husband and children read the pride and encouragement in my gestures when they've accomplished a goal. I clap. I smile. I offer a thumbs up or a big hug.

I'm aware my face is expressive, and if I'm sending an uninviting signal, I can halt a conversation. Therefore, I try to keep my facial expressions and other body language neutral when appropriate, especially when talking about hard topics. Otherwise, I may inadvertently steer the discussion in a harmful direction.

Body language can be misunderstood. People typically cross their arms because they're closed to an idea, want to be excluded from a discussion, or disagree with an opinion. But sometimes people cross their arms because they're physically cold and they're simply warming themselves. Sometimes my stance is misread. I can be engrossed in thought, mentally checking my long to-do list and determining my next task when someone asks me what's wrong.

Be aware of signals—those sent and those received. Sometimes clarification is necessary before proceeding with a conversation.

Use Appropriate Touch

Years ago, while I was attending a class for moms to be, a facilitator demonstrated how touch relaxes people. She asked a mom to stand up, and she slowly and lightly ran her hands down the volunteer's right arm, starting at her shoulder and ending at her fingertips. When she finished, the mom's entire right side was visibly more relaxed than the untouched side.

Touch disarms. I can be mad and shouting at my husband, but if he folds me into his arms (kudos to him for doing this while I'm yelling), I melt. I drop my shield of anger and begin revealing the emotions behind the anger. We may not solve our problem right away, but the discussion becomes more productive.

With few exceptions (yes, I know of people who bristle at someone else's touch), sitting close and touching someone lowers their defenses. When you need to chat with your children about an uncomfortable subject, try sitting next to them and briefly touching their arm or leg. This gesture is reassuring to them and helpful to you. It's hard to raise your voice when you are touching the other person. Of course, if it's awkward, let go. Use discernment so your actions don't move from comforting to creepy.

Sometimes, Words Are Necessary

My husband and children *can't* read my mind. Okay, I get it. But I sometimes send signals that go undetected. If I allow it, this frustrates me, especially when my husband and I are out with friends and I don't want to say what I'm thinking. Don't we love phones because of this? If I'm not fond of the meal and don't want to be put on the spot, I text my husband, "Don't ask me if I like the food."

Some people are more intuitive than others and naturally pick up on body language, code words, or small hints. This trait is especially helpful in a group. When facilitating at school or leading a connection group at church, I try to read the room, scanning and interpreting as I teach or listen. However, not everyone possesses this perceptive ability.

Those who express themselves with subtle body language and facial expressions may need to practice using words when necessary. My husband and I serve on a team at church together. I used to expect him to watch for my signals, interpret them, and then state my opinions to the group. As I write that expectation, I realize how silly it sounds. I feared I wouldn't voice my thoughts properly or my opinions would be rejected; thus, they were rejecting me. I believed if my husband articulated the message instead of me, it would be warmly received. Unfortunately, he didn't always pick up on my signal or communicate the message accurately. I'm braver now. When I have a thought, I say it. I'm learning to speak without my inflection or tone betraying my fear.

As parents, let's drop the expectation that our children possess the ability to convey messages without their feelings convoluting their intended meaning. Let's encourage them to speak through their fear, hurt, anger, and sadness. Then, when their emotions settle and the conversation is light, we can coach them on how to calmly state their concerns and opinions.

> Let's drop the expectation that our children possess the ability to convey messages without their feelings convoluting their intended meaning.

Pay Attention to Tone and Inflection
How we say what we say is important. A high, soft pitch sounds sweeter than a low, loud pitch. Although, depending on normal

voice level, it may sound fake. When interacting, consider how the inflection of a voice rises and falls, as well as the cadence of the words and syllables. A monotone sound and staccato rhythm may appear uncaring. Conversely, when the volume escalates, it exposes anger or frustration.

Pray Together

Jesus says, "For where two or three gather in my name, there am I with them" (Matt. 18:20). Praying with others is humbling. It exposes vulnerabilities, breaks down walls, and softens hearts. Prayer is a necessary component in all relationships, but especially with our children. Prayer demonstrates we're willing to subject our lives to God, who we recognize as our chief authority. Prayer reminds us and our children that God is for us, with us, and in us. We model prayer because, as they mature, we want the next generation to rely less on us and more on him.

In your prayers, pray for a resolution to the issue at hand, the strength to walk through the process, and a more cohesive relationship with him and each other. Ask God to be the focus and center of the relationship. Thank him for who he is and for his refining and redemptive power.

Put It All Together

Being cognizant of the various elements involved in conversation and connection helps us transmit our *intended* message, especially when delving into difficult conversations. If we aren't careful, our tone, body language, and emotions will push others away. If those around us detect anger, disappointment, or indifference, they may shut down before we articulate our ideas. But prioritizing the relationship, being open to listening, pausing for reflection, and releasing the results to God allow the relationship to flourish.

Difficult Conversations

By this point, you may be wondering how to begin a difficult conversation, one that encompasses the topics we let fall through the cracks—the embarrassing subjects. How do we begin discussions regarding sex, sexuality, pornography, masturbation, hookups, sending and receiving nudes, and all things online? If there was ever a time in which parents were exploring unfamiliar terrain, this is it. Widespread usage of smartphones is a fairly recent phenomenon, so we can't ask our parents and grandparents for advice. We're learning as we go.

We can no longer wait until our children hit puberty before discussing these important issues. Those talks now need to begin at a young age and before we hand them a device that connects to the Internet. Our objective is to normalize the conversation so, as our children mature, ongoing conversations aren't awkward or out of place. They are, well, normal. We hope our children receive our wisdom related to these topics as they would our advice on washing behind their ears, learning to tie their shoes, or riding a bicycle.

But what if our children are already preteens, teens, or young adults? Can we still broach these topics? Yep! It's not too late. Most children, regardless of age, crave connection with their parents or another trusted adult and will listen to their advice, although they may not act like they care.

The best way to break the invisible barrier, to bash the stigma saying these discussions are off limits, is to simply walk through the awkward moment and bring them up.

My coworkers and I were in a class of ninth graders at a local school. On the first day of the twelve sessions, we were illustrating why it's important to allow our emotions some space before making decisions.

"We want the logical portion of our brain, not our emotions, to control our behavior," I said. "For example, lonely people may become desperate for friends. What would happen if a teen who is allowing feelings of loneliness to control their decisions is invited by a peer to a party with drinking, vaping, and watching pornography?"

"What?!" one student blurted.

Another giggled. One blushed. A girl put her head between her hands. Two guys looked at each other as if to say: *Did she just say what I thought she said?*

"That's right," I continued. "I use that word. We'll discuss sex and pornography more in-depth in later sessions. For now, let's get back to our lonely person. When we allow emotions, like loneliness or sadness, to drive our actions, we're more apt to join friends in these types of risky behaviors."

I wasn't trying to shock them with my abrupt use of the word *pornography*. Instead, I introduced it on our first day together to indicate we were going to broach hard topics, ones not typically discussed by teachers or authority figures.

As a sexual risk avoidance specialist, I'm accustomed to using these words, but it took *a lot* of practice. If you need to, pick a few awkward words to add to your vocabulary and practice saying them out loud in front of a mirror. Then approach your child and request a time to chat about an important subject. Here are a few samples to help you get started:

"I recently heard the average age of exposure to pornography is between eight and eleven. I'd like to hear your thoughts on it. Can we set a time to talk?"

"I don't believe I've done a great job talking with you about sex and sexuality. I'm so sorry I haven't covered this topic as thoroughly as I should have. Let's set aside a few minutes to talk in the next day or two."

"I recently read the definition of a hookup. Do you know anything about hookup culture? I'd love to hear your thoughts."

"Wow. I just found out how teens are finding pornography through gaming. I didn't realize that was a thing. What do you know about it?"

"I just learned that sending and receiving nudes starts in middle school. What can you tell me about it?"

The objective of the initial conversation is to open the door to these discussions, not push an agenda. While we eventually want to express our thoughts, opinions, and position to our teens, if we start by telling them what to do, they won't be as eager to ask questions or seek our help when they're struggling. We want the door to these subjects to stay open.

If you've been closed off or haven't addressed these issues thoroughly enough, admit it. If you've already learned of inappropriate behavior and mishandled the conversations, it's okay. Apologize, and state you want to do a better job of protecting them and keeping them informed. Ask your children how you can best help them. Teens have brilliant ideas. Most appreciate when we ask, and they willingly share.

The goal is building and preserving healthy relationships with our children. Do we want their decisions to reflect God's standards? Yes. But if we focus specifically on changing behaviors, persuading them to bend their actions to our will, they may walk the straight and narrow for a time, for our benefit, to please us. However, they are less likely to adopt the underlying beliefs and are more likely to rebel later. When we focus on maintaining a strong relationship, one that includes connection, bonding, mutuality, and trust, we foster an environment in which our teens feel comfortable talking about anything and everything. They will then trust our judgment and listen to our rationale.

> When we focus on maintaining a strong relationship, one that includes connection, bonding, mutuality, and trust, we foster an environment in which our teens feel comfortable talking about anything and everything.

Remember to read the Bible and assess your beliefs regarding God's purpose for sex (see Chapter Four). Then continue talking about sex and related topics. If you read a statistic, share it. If you see a sensual scene while watching a show, ask their opinion about the scene and how it makes them feel. While riding in the car, ask an open-ended question related to peer pressure or the latest trend on social media.

Put yourself in their shoes, and look at the world from their perspective. If you sense resistance, try a different approach next time. We want to break down barriers hindering the relationship. If you've held your child at arm's length, resented them, or clashed because of personality differences or behavior problems, apologize for not expressing unconditional love. As parents/caregivers, it's our move—our job—to remove the bricks that created the wall between us and our children. Granted, our teens may lay those bricks faster than we can remove them, but we should strive to keep that wall short. Let's create an atmosphere of understanding, sympathy, and compassion because our hope is that they will trust us—if not now, someday.

Relate to them through vulnerability. Share personal stories from your past, leaving out details. The next generation thinks their struggles with insecurity, temptation, and emotional turmoil are abnormal. They need us to confirm they are not alone. Preteens, teens, and young adults (where does it end, really?) grapple with emotional ups and downs, feelings of hurt and rejection, and the desire to fit in with peers. Each of us is relieved when we realize we aren't the only ones battling these thoughts and emotions.

The trick for us parents is to be authentic and real without appearing needy. When possible, share from a place of healing, not from a place of hurt.

As the conversations progress, remember that your teens are priceless children of God and are created in his image. Treat them accordingly. Show unconditional love and acceptance. Validate their thoughts and opinions. Consider their needs and long-ings (see Chapter Four). Ask questions, clarify their responses, and reflect their ideas and feelings back to them. One method for doing this is to state, "What I hear you saying is that when this _____ (action) _____ took place, you thought _____ and felt _____. Did I hear you correctly?" This mirroring is a tool to ensure you comprehend their message correctly before responding, not an indication you agree with their assessment. After replying, ask them to mirror the message back to you for the same purpose.

Consent

Consent is another hot topic. The legal definition of consent, including age of consent for sexual activity, varies from state to state within the United States. But no matter the legalities, the principle behind the topic is important to discuss. All parties should feel comfortable and safe within the confines of a rela-tionship, whether holding hands or having intercourse. Each should be mature enough to use correct terminology and have a detailed conversation.

The aim is for one person in the relationship to ask a specific question: *Is it okay if I put my hand here? Are you ready to have intercourse?* The second person must verbally answer *yes* for it to be considered consent. But, this person can later say that they didn't really mean it. So sometimes even *yes* is not consent. Ideally, both parties will give an enthusiastic *yes* before progressing.

Silence is not consent. Passivity is not consent. A cute smile is not consent. Someone who has been drinking or taking drugs (including certain prescription drugs) cannot give consent.

Unfortunately, many young adults are uncomfortable telling a partner *no* when progressing through the steps of intimacy. They either say *okay* to avoid a confrontation or rejection, or they stay silent. This lack of communication is interpreted as consent. Although assault is not limited to females, our sons especially should learn to ask questions and be respectful of their partners' answers. This is biblical, *and* it keeps them from being accused of sexual assault.

As we discussed in Chapter Five, setting and communicating boundaries may deter some awkward moments. But even within marriages, asking questions is fitting. Not only are questions and discussions regarding likes and dislikes considerate, but they help couples learn how to please each other physically, as well as bond emotionally. Teaching our children to express themselves prepares them to enjoy intimacy after they're married.

Tread Lightly

As we've explored throughout this book, incorrect and fabricated messages are dispatched constantly. Our children are bombarded with misleading and erroneous information. Negotiating a conversation with a teen we believe is wrong or under a false impression is an arduous task. Helping children distinguish between fact and fiction, especially when they don't want assistance, is a complex job.

When do we speak up? When do we stay silent? When do we intervene? When do we compromise? These are all fabulous questions with no one-size-fits-all answers. Each unique relationship requires unique interactions. Each one-of-a-kind circumstance requires a one-of-a-kind response. This is evidence of our need for the Holy Spirit.

When sensing a desire to counter a belief or disagree with your teens' conclusion, tread lightly. In general, teens don't like being told what to do or how to think. (Who does?) Try asking questions. Why do you think Steve asked you for a nude? What was his motive? What are your options? If you choose not to send one, how will that affect the relationship? How did his request make you feel?

When our teens' beliefs don't line up with God's Word, we may ask them: What do you think God says about it? Do you agree with Scripture on that subject? What is motivating you? We hope to affect their thoughts and opinions, to redirect them toward scriptural truth, without dictating their behaviors.

Yes, they live in our home. Yes, they need to live according to our rules. Yes, we have final say. I'm not negating that sentiment. I'm attempting to cultivate a long-lasting relationship. Are there times when *because I said so* trumps their out-of-control behavior patterns? Yes. But, as one who has abused the *because I said so* stance in the past, I fear we aren't equipping our teens to relate well to others in the future or make healthy decisions on their own. When we guide them toward godly decisions, we are planting seeds, nurturing their reasoning skills, and reminding them that God is trustworthy.

A loving relationship with a fulfilling sex life requires interest, mutual respect, understanding, and reciprocity by both parties. This back and forth appears to be lacking in hookup culture, which primarily benefits males and leaves females wanting for more.

God created both men and women to enjoy sexual activity. When discussing sex, mention the positive aspects. As bodies develop and mature, preteens and teens feel attraction and desire. That's normal. When hormones kick in, their bodies are functioning properly, the way God intended. But, until it's appropriate to act on those bodily responses and feelings, we want them to exercise self-control.

Yet what if they don't? And what if they've already stumbled?

Offer Grace

If our children send nudes, watch pornography, have sex, or participate in other unhealthy behaviors, they're probably experiencing shame and guilt. They may believe we'd view them as used or blemished if they confessed. We don't want to add to their negative self-image.

While talking, admit you don't have all the answers and aren't able to disseminate information flawlessly. Therefore, you don't expect them to be perfect. Just like you have faltered, failed, and sinned, they will, too. But we have grace through the blood of Christ. When we confess, he purifies us. In his eyes, we are blameless. Our past doesn't decree our future. He allows for do-overs.

> Our past doesn't decree our future. He allows for do-overs.

Remind your children, from when they are infants to adults, that you love them unconditionally, are on their side, and desire to walk beside them through life. Tell them your goal is for them to be the best version of themselves, to thrive and live a long, fulfilling life.

Parents, we have an amazing job. We are affecting the next generation. We are molding them into self-sufficient adults. Let's empower our children by giving them a voice, to speak up—to us, their friends, partners, and the world. Let's help them by offering them the skills, characteristics, and healthy habits necessary to succeed. They will be world changers.

recovery and restoration

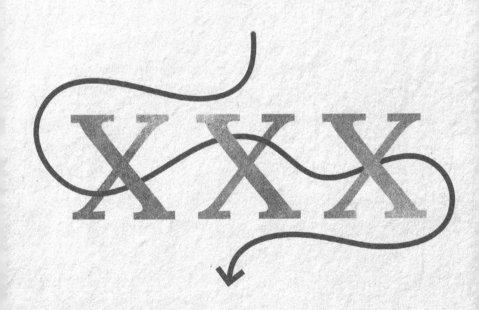

CHAPTER
7

Healing from Wounds

Praise the LORD, my soul;
all my inmost being, praise his holy name.
Praise the LORD, my soul,
and forget not all his benefits—
who forgives all your sins
and heals all your diseases,
who redeems your life from the pit
and crowns you with love and compassion,
who satisfies your desires with good things
so that your youth is renewed like the eagle's.

(Ps. 103:1–5)

I looked at my phone. My son was calling. "Hello."

"Mrs. Winters? We're at the trampoline park, and—"

"Who is this?"

"Oh, sorry." It was my son's girlfriend. "We were jumping on a trampoline, and now he's stuck in a pit."

"What?!" I visualized a deep, narrow, dark hole with my son at the bottom, desperately reaching up, unable to climb to the top on his own.

"We heard a loud sound, and he thinks he broke his leg."

My husband and I were an hour and a half away. My son, weeks from starting his senior year of high school, lay in a ball pit (ah! that kind of pit) with his leg twisted out of place. Thankfully, an EMT was onsite. After assessing the situation, he called an ambulance.

When Don and I arrived at the ER, we only saw him a few minutes before medical personnel ushered us out of the room. From the hall, I heard my son scream as they set his leg. He was losing circulation to his foot, and they couldn't wait for the pain medication to take effect. He would have lost his foot had they not acted quickly. My husband held me as we cried and prayed. That was one of the longest minutes of my life.

After he was out of immediate danger, we had decisions. The X-ray showed clean breaks through his tibia and fibula (both of the bones between the knee and foot). Because he was seventeen and possibly still growing, we had options for treatment. We listened to the advice of professionals, prayed fervently, and made a choice. My concern, however, was that the surgery we selected would debilitate him for the rest of his life. If we chose incorrectly, it was possible he would not walk or throw the javelin again. It could have been my fault if he did not regain as much wholeness as possible.

Wounds

One of our biggest fears as parents and caregivers, apart from losing a child, is that our children will suffer from some traumatic event, issue, or addiction they won't recover from. Therefore, they could be mentally, emotionally, physically, or spiritually disabled, so to speak. Their holistic well-being could be compromised, leaving them limping, impaired, and less than for the rest of their lives. We want our children to succeed and thrive, *to be happy*, to borrow a portion of the phrase from Chapter One.

No matter when our children face a challenging situation, infant to eighty, we support them and root for them. But when the trauma, issue, problem, or addiction takes place in our home, under our roof, while they're in our care, their dilemma becomes our dilemma. Our fears escalate because we have a personal responsibility. What if we try our hardest and they don't mend? What if we offer the wrong advice and mess them up for life? What if we treat the figurative wound improperly? These decisions weigh on us. We take them seriously by listing all our choices and praying. But sometimes it feels like we're trying to hit a target while blindfolded. That's how I felt the night we chose the surgery that would leave my son with a fourteen-inch rod in his leg for the rest of his life.

Our calling as parents, grandparents, or caregivers is to stand by, make the tough decisions, and pray that God uses our words, actions, and intentions for his glory.

When our children are younger, we have more authority, responsibility, influence, and control. As they mature, however, the burden of healthy decisions shifts to their shoulders. Yes, we need to be there, to help them and guide them. Whether they recognize it or not, our role is still vital in their lives. But the fallout of their decisions is theirs to bear. So, we adjust our interactions as they change and our relationship develops. We remain fluid, adapting to the situation at hand.

Our children will make choices they regret. They will fail us and themselves. They will ignore God's Word and blatantly sin. They will try their hardest and fall, because they're human. It's ridiculous for us to assume we can tell them once and they'll listen, grasp the lesson, and follow our directions every time. We don't behave perfectly. We can't. Neither can they.

What if we've done our best (or not) and our teen or young adult watched pornography? Or developed an addiction? What if we can't pry the device out of their hands? Or they were pressured into sending a nude? Or they believe sending and receiving nudes is no big deal? What if they're involved in hookup culture? How do we help them heal?

And what about the wounds we carry because of our children's pain, shame, and hurtful behavior? How do *we* heal?

For the rest of this chapter, we'll look at personal healing, both for our children and for us. Then, in the last chapter, we'll talk about mending relationships.

The Great Physician

Whether we're processing through an issue of our own making or dealing with the effects of someone else's unhealthy choices, the primary answer is the same: Jesus. Each of us walks through injuries and offenses separately and uniquely, but the individualized path is crafted by Jesus. As believers, we can confidently approach the throne of grace for forgiveness, healing, and correction.

> Whether we're processing through an issue of our own making or dealing with the effects of someone else's unhealthy choices, the primary answer is the same: Jesus.

Therefore, since we have a great high priest who has
ascended into heaven, Jesus the Son of God, let us hold
firmly to the faith we profess. For we do not have a high
priest who is unable to empathize with our weaknesses,
but we have one who has been tempted in every way,
just as we are—yet he did not sin. Let us then approach
God's throne of grace with confidence, so that we may
receive mercy and find grace to help us in our time of
need. (Heb. 4:14–16)

Notice that Jesus empathizes with our weaknesses because he
experienced temptation. And, while he did not sin, he under-
stands our turmoil. When we approach him in our time of need,
he offers his mercy and grace.

Whatever our problems or concerns, our first step is to pray,
to take the mess to God. When we learn of our teen's indiscretions
or realize our own behaviors need addressed, our inclination is to
attack the problem with full force. Sometimes, this creates a bigger
crisis. It's okay to wait before developing a plan of action.

If you're realizing you've made unhealthy choices recently
or in the past, attend to them. However, for now, I'm assuming
you're a parent, grandparent, guardian, caregiver, or trusted adult
of a teen or young adult who has been involved in some type of
sexually deviant behavior, such as hookups, pornography, or pre-
marital sex.

When a teen confesses to sending and receiving nudes, is
caught in a possible coercion situation, has been watching pornography, or fill in the blank, try not to react by throwing out devices
or changing all the rules. Instead, thank your child for trusting you

with the information, listen to them, and take time to pray about your response. If appropriate, pray with your teen.

As Jesus empathizes with us, we can interact with our children with empathy. Now is the time to put the communication tips offered in Chapter Six into practice. If you're already past the initial conversation and feel like you messed up, it's okay. Apologize and start again.

When you're ready, after you've sat with Jesus and asked for guidance, talk with your teen. Start by reassuring them of your unconditional love and desire to help. They may feel shame and guilt. Shame is a powerful force. Point out that guilt, or conviction, is a gift from God, but shame, the belief that one is a bad person, is a false identity. When shameful behaviors and emotions are exposed to the light by talking about them, it weakens their power.

Tackle the Behavior

Discuss ways to set boundaries to help change unwanted behavior. Elicit their advice. Ask if God revealed any specific steps to them. Consider:

- Assessing their level of involvement with the behavior (e.g., Is this an addiction, obsession, habit, or casual behavior?)
- Adding filters to the Wi-Fi and devices
- Using parental controls (these can be effective even for adults)
- Revising eating, exercise, and sleep habits
- Scheduling daily check-ins
- Researching dangers

- Updating rules regarding screen time, curfew, and devices in bedrooms and bathrooms
- Deleting some or all social media apps
- Limiting alone time
- Limiting time with friends
- Evaluating friendships (Are these friends positive influences?)
- Setting short-term and long-term goals
- Talking with a professional

This list is not exhaustive. Explore outside circumstances and internal promptings. We will look at a few of those more in-depth as we continue our discussion.

We Can't Change Them

There's a saying: you can lead a horse to water, but you can't make him drink. Of course, we can't force a horse to drink. But if we own the horse, we don't ignore him or give up on him. We guide the horse to the stream, the source, to quench his thirst. If he doesn't drink, we lead him into the stream or entice him with a bucket of flavored water. We help him comprehend his thirst, his need for water.

Unfortunately, we can't force our teens or young adult children to change their behaviors. We can encourage, support, influence, and cheer them on. We can inform, yell, and prompt. We can even threaten and bribe. But we can't make them change. We can't do it for them. They must want to change. The desire must come from within. It must be intrinsic.

My husband and I held our son's hand in the ER after he broke his leg. We chose the surgery we believed was the best. I slept in the makeshift bed next to his in the hospital. I filled the prescriptions and cooked him chicken noodle soup during his recovery. I even drove him to school and back for weeks. But I could not relearn to walk for him. I couldn't perform the physical therapy. I couldn't change his desire to walk again. He had to want it on his own. Thankfully, he *wanted* to walk again. And he did. Then he ran. Then he was back on the field throwing the javelin. He worked through the obstacles and endured the pain and frustrations because he had a goal and an internal craving to meet the goal.

Distinguishing our part from our children's is important. Our role is to help our children heal without carrying responsibilities that aren't ours or adopting false guilt when they don't succeed.

Some of us fear hurting our children or pushing them away with our boldness or our timidity. Then our paralysis keeps us from staying the course, from continuing the strenuous task of walking with our children through their recovery process. Paul encourages us in his second letter to the Corinthians.

> Even if I caused you sorrow by my letter, I do not regret it. Though I did regret it—I see that my letter hurt you, but only for a little while—yet now I am happy, not because you were made sorry, but because your sorrow led you to repentance. For you became sorrowful as God intended and so were not harmed in any way by us. Godly sorrow brings repentance that leads to salvation and leaves no regret, but worldly sorrow brings death. See what this godly sorrow has produced in you: what earnestness, what eagerness to clear yourselves, what indignation, what alarm, what longing, what concern,

what readiness to see justice done. At every point you
have proved yourselves to be innocent in this matter.
(2 Cor. 7:8–11)

Paul was grateful he wrote his first letter to the Corinthians, even
though it initially caused pain, because his message ignited sorrow,
which led to repentance. Discussions with our children can be
awkward, even painful. But these crucial moments can induce a
godly sorrow—an intrinsic motivation to look within, evaluate
behaviors, repent, and choose a healthier path. Worldly sorrow
is extrinsic and leads to death. Godly sorrow leads to life. That's
our heart's cry.

> Worldly sorrow is extrinsic and leads to
> death. Godly sorrow leads to life.

Intrinsic Motivation

My son, who struggled with a pornography addiction, has the
following to say about intrinsic motivation:

> Leon Festinger, an influential psychologist, developed
> the theory of cognitive dissonance, the discomfort felt
> by individuals when their beliefs are not consistent
> with their actions. According to Festinger, a person
> resolves the dissonance in one of three ways: changing
> their behavior, changing their belief, or justifying their
> actions by reducing their belief.
>
> So how did I resolve my cognitive dissonance when
> I found myself, a pastor's son who prided himself on his
> upstanding behavior, addicted to pornography?

Before I answer, let me provide some background information. I was first exposed to pornography at around the age of ten and struggled with it for about eight years, on and off. The first year or so, I didn't know what I was doing was wrong. I knew my parents wouldn't appreciate my actions, but I didn't understand the gravity of the situation as a whole. It was after I understood my actions were immoral for reasons outside my parents' beliefs that I truly experienced cognitive dissonance.

What were my options to alleviate this dissonance?

1. Change my behavior. I would need to quit watching pornography.
2. Change my beliefs. I would need to find information to match my actions. For example, I may conclude from my research: *the Bible doesn't actually condemn pornography* or *pornography doesn't really promote sex trafficking.*
3. Justify my actions by reducing the importance of the dissonance. This would involve me believing something like, *Everyone does it, so it's not really a big deal.*

I found myself in this last category for a while. I figured since watching pornography was normal, I shouldn't feel guilty. This viewpoint only did the trick for a couple of years, though.

I experienced the discomfort of dissonance once again. So, I finally told my parents about the struggle. When I informed them, however, I wasn't really interested in getting better. I simply told them because I felt I needed to. My confession was halfhearted.

Due to lack of intrinsic motivation, this "freedom" from porn was short-lived, and I soon fell back into the same situation. This time, though, the dissonance was much worse. I was more informed of the harmful effects of pornography, had a girlfriend, and was lying to my parents on a daily basis. I was dying inside.

The day came when I, once again, went to my parents to confess I was still watching pornography. It was one of the most difficult things I have done. I could no longer claim I was young and ignorant or fall back on my sweet, charming innocence. I told my parents I'd been lying to them. I hated doing it, but I knew I had to if I ever wanted to get better.

Luckily, my parents were kind and accepting of me. I believe this is one of the best things parents can do for their children. Children will never confess to their parents if they believe the wrath of their parents will be worse than the reward of getting help. My parents put heavy restrictions on all devices. It was tough, but it was what I needed.

I would be lying if I said I never struggled with pornography or lust again, but I fought honestly every day. I haven't watched pornography in a long period of time, and I owe my success to many people. My parents significantly helped me get through that fight. My youth leader and some friends helped me a great deal. Mostly, I owe it to God. I didn't experience true freedom until I gave up everything in my life to him and quit trying to hold on.

To ultimately and finally resolve my cognitive dissonance, I changed my behavior. I believe this is the only way someone struggling with pornography will ever experience genuine relief.

It is important to note that, although cognitive dissonance is uncomfortable, in this case, it's still good. It forces the person who experiences it to make one of the three above-mentioned decisions. Our job, now, is to encourage people to make the freeing decision to alter their behavior, and then help them change by encouraging them and showing them love.

Triggers

Once our children are ready to change, when it's their idea to begin the healing process, we can walk with them and offer emotional support and words of wisdom along the way. Listen to their suggestions. Modify external circumstances, like household rules. But also, help discover the underlying cause of the behavior. What was their initial motive? Curiosity? Excitement? Lack of understanding? Peer pressure? Deception? An unfilled need or longing (refer to Chapter Four)? Be patient as you explore the answers. They may not know why they took that first step.

Determine why the behavior continued. Did they crave those dopamine hits? Were they trying to fit in? Would others make fun of them or bully them if they resisted hookup culture, sending nudes, or other activities viewed as normal and acceptable? Are they addicted? (If this is the case, a detox program may be necessary.)

As your conversations progress, attempt to uncover triggers— stimuli that prompt them to engage in the harmful behavior. Once they've identified their triggers, they're better armed to combat them.

As your conversations progress, attempt to uncover triggers—
stimuli that prompt them to engage in the harmful behavior.

Triggers can be psychological or situational.

A common acronym used for psychological triggers is BLAST (bored, lonely, angry, stressed, tired).

Bored

My son originally sought pornography out of curiosity, but one reason he returned to it was boredom. To counterattack this trigger, we wrote a list of activities for him to choose from when he was bored. He also began research projects and pursued new hobbies.

When he first started his recovery program, we scheduled his day with no downtime. Later, he learned how to fill in those gaps of boredom with Bible reading, prayer, and other quieting thoughts.

Lonely

When the need to belong is not met, teens feel lonely. Lonely people search for ways to connect with others, boost their self-esteem, or otherwise cope. As with other triggers, our children may fill the emptiness by self-medicating—eating, sleeping, using alcohol or drugs, hooking up, scrolling mindlessly through social media, playing games for hours on end, or watching pornography. And, remember from Chapter Three, teens with unfilled longings are more susceptible to online grooming for human trafficking.

We can add "being alone" to this category. There is a difference between the two, as someone who is alone may not be lonely. But being by oneself offers an opportunity to pursue behaviors not considered in the company of others.

My son cited being alone as a trigger for watching pornography. As part of his treatment, we agreed with his request for constant companionship. Other than sleeping, he stayed in the main part of the house when we were home and tagged along when we left the house.

Angry

Angry people make poor decisions, especially if the situation is out of their control. The amygdala—the irrational, emotional portion of the brain—takes over. The instinct may be to run to the activity bringing immediate relief, even if it's only a short-term fix and won't bring long-term fulfillment or enjoyment.

Stressed

Our teens experience an extreme amount of internal and external pressure to perform at a certain level, to behave a particular way, and to fit in with classmates. This causes stress and anxiety. As with anger, when nervous, worried, or fearful, the amygdala kicks into overdrive. The desire is to find a quick path out of the anxious situation, to ease the discomfort and calm their nerves as quickly as possible.

Tired

Tired people can be moody and make illogical decisions. A sleep-deprived person may be desperate for a relaxation technique and turn to unhealthy methods like drugs or alcohol. Many who struggle with pornography rely on the chemical release of an orgasm to help them sleep. The body becomes accustomed to this habit.

Hungry

Let's examine one more psychological trigger. As with all triggers, one false move can send a hungry person spiraling into a pattern of negative choices. Someone who's hungry may snap at a family member. That, then, instigates a back and forth between the two or a sense of guilt in the "snapper." From there, they may self-soothe with their vice of choice.

Situational Triggers

Psychological triggers are based on inner longings or needs, but situational triggers develop from outside sources or conditions. Most of us, for example, routinely eat supper at the same time each night. If we're unable to grab our meal at the designated time, our bodies remind us that it's time to eat.

The same can be true for those caught in pornography, hookups, gaming, social media scrolling, or any type of addiction. For example, if a young adult has attended a hookup party every weekend for a year, she may subconsciously check her social media at 8:00 p.m. on a Friday for the location of that night's party, dress in a specific outfit, and begin the preparty routine of downing shots of vodka. Her behavior is automatic. One step leads to the next. She doesn't stop to think about the consequences of her behavior, and before she realizes, she wakes up in someone else's bed the next morning.

A specific friend could be a trigger. A sexual scene on a streaming app may be triggering. A particular time of day or certain atmosphere, a word or phrase, or a smell or taste could activate a desire to seek relief in the addictive behavior. Our minds and bodies learn and instinctually respond consistently to certain situations. The brain is wired, or rewired, to function in a particular manner. It's formed those grooves referred to in Chapter One.

Areas of Life

Some of us were taught that all issues are spiritual and fought through prayer and spiritual warfare. I'm not minimizing the spiritual element. I agree it's the most important part of who we are. However, we cannot disregard or downplay the physical, chemical, hormonal, emotional, psychological, relational, and situational components of our lives. God created us. He composed each of us and designed our bodies and minds. These other components are real and worth tending to.

> We cannot disregard or downplay the physical, chemical, hormonal, emotional, psychological, relational, and situational components of our lives.

Your Triggers

Whether you are a mom, dad, grandparent, guardian, or caregiver, you probably have triggers, too. While our discussion has primarily focused on our teens' triggers, think about conditions or emotions that push *your* buttons, causing you to panic, get angry, or want to escape. For example, a few months into my son's treatment, he stayed home alone for the first time. My heart raced when I left. My instinct was to run back into the house and tell him he had to come with me. I recognized the impulse as an irrational thought born of fear and forced myself to continue with my plans.

How Do We Pinpoint Triggers?

Ask God to reveal them. Then pay attention. When you or your child sense anxiety, pain, fear, depression, shame, or anger and want to reach for an unhealthy quick fix, think about the event, circumstance, or emotion that instigated (triggered) the unwanted desire. Identifying the trigger, exposing the stimulant, is a critical first step in counteracting it.

How Do We Respond to Triggers?

To rewire our brains to lean on God and his provision rather than outside stimuli or images filed away in our minds, we have options. Again, we are complex individuals, so what may "work" for one person may not for another. God doesn't provide a fool-proof formula.

When creating a plan, consider the following:

- ▶ Breathe. Find a method of relaxation that works for you. We want to allow space for the reasoning portion of the brain to take control.
- ▶ Enjoy a change of scenery. Leave the place that instigates the unwanted behavior.
- ▶ Move around. Get up. Stretch. Go outside. Exercise. Physical activity activates a different portion of the brain and suppresses anxious thoughts.
- ▶ Practice self-care. Eat well, exercise, and get plenty of sleep. Take breaks from stressful situations.
- ▶ Evaluate sleep patterns. Recondition your mind and body to sleep seven to nine hours in a row. Go to bed and get up at the same time each day. If you wake up in the middle of the night, stay in bed.
- ▶ Compile a list of activities. Refer to this list when bored. Examples of items to include: ride a bike, work a puzzle, read a book, write, listen to music or a podcast, do home-work, cook, clean, visit a museum, start a new project.

- Modify household rules, as needed. I listed some suggestions earlier in the chapter.
- Update personal boundaries or limits. For example, a teen may choose not to hold hands with anyone for a period of time because it's a gateway to more sexual activity.
- Schedule ongoing conversations. Check in with your child regularly. The conversation may be short, but it reminds them you care and are willing to talk about the issue. Check-ins are also a form of accountability.
- Find a friend. Both parents and children need friends to talk with about their problems.
- Seek professional help. Seek help from a professional when necessary.
- Research other suggestions as needed.

Collateral Damage

What about those of us standing beside the one making unhealthy choices, those of us affected by the results of their behavior? Parents, siblings, and friends feel the consequences of those directly involved. Their missteps splatter us with residual effects.

Betrayal Trauma

When my son's indiscretions surfaced, I felt like I'd been punched in the gut and then kicked while down. I was unknowingly in a war zone, and when the bomb exploded, I was hit. The fallout of his conduct landed on me.

I hadn't caught him in a lie before, so I couldn't believe my son had snuck around behind my back and lied to me without any indication. This information, that my son disregarded our relationship and purposefully deceived me, was more shocking than his pornography use confession. I suffered from betrayal trauma.

It's natural to react physically and emotionally when hearing of a loved one's transgressions. Depending on the length and depth of the behavior and our level of ignorance regarding it, our minds and bodies may respond as they would to any trauma. Our emotions go into overdrive, protecting ourselves. We may experience the fight-or-flight syndrome with a gut instinct to throw everything we've got at the problem or escape. The damage caused by the incident is compounded by our loved one's betrayal.

Grief

I also experienced grief. We typically associate grief with a physical death. However, the day I discovered my son watched pornography, I lost the son I knew. He was replaced by a stranger, someone who lied, deceived, and participated in behavior I didn't think was possible. Not only was his past different than I knew it to be, but his future would be as well. As I managed our situation and navigated this parenting endeavor, I walked through all the stages of grief—denial, anger, bargaining, depression, and, eventually, acceptance.

Grieving is a long but necessary process. We don't sail through each stage at the same pace or in a linear direction. We may be in denial one day, depressed the next, and feel anger the following three days. That's okay.

Look at your situation and evaluate if you are grieving. If so, lean into God and allow him to comfort you through it. "Blessed are those who mourn, for they will be comforted" (Matt. 5:4).

It's Not Personal

We're apt to assume our children think about the ramifications of their actions and how those consequences affect those around them. If they've disregarded our advice, we believe they've purposefully rebelled against us. In our minds, we see our children rationally thinking through all their choices and picking the one that angers us the most because they don't believe us and are out to get us.

Yet, in most cases, their decisions have nothing to do with us. It's not personal. As we've discussed, they're motivated by curiosity or a perceived or real need. Then once they're trapped in the behavior, their cravings take over. They have no control. When we realize their choices aren't a personal attack on us, we are offended less, we are angered less, and forgiving is easier.

Treat Your Wounds

Whether feeling the effects of betrayal trauma, grief, or both, we don't want to ignore our emotions or disregard the deep pain inflicted by our children. These effects exist and need attention.

Allowing God to tend our wounds while continuing to parent our children and manage their distresses is a demanding task. We don't want our hurts to impede our children's healing process. At the same time, we want to remain authentic. I've said to my son, "I'm hurt, but I'll get over it. Please continue to trust me, confide in me, and tell me your needs. I'll do my best to be available. Don't hide things from me just because I might not like what you have to say. It's not your job to protect me."

Why Pursue Healing?

Six weeks after his surgery, my son sat on the couch and pedaled the stationary mini exercise bike we purchased for his physical therapy. He worked through the pain that still pestered him. Even though his leg, ankle, and knee hurt to move, he knew the bones, muscles, and ligaments would not heal and would not perform properly if he didn't persevere. He had a goal: to compete at the state track meet in six months. He focused on the end goal and took the steps necessary to meet the goal. When he had a setback, he started again. He persisted, disciplining himself to continue, because he knew the long hours of physical therapy were beneficial for his overall well-being and essential for obtaining his goal.

As you and your child pursue wellness, ask God to reveal triggers and other wounded areas—places of hurt or offense. Adapt and revise rules or behaviors, as needed, for recovery to transpire, and pay attention to the spiritual aspect of treatment. Allow God in. He is the one who renews minds and retrains thinking.

Let's return to the information from Chapter One regarding the pliability of the brain. A person performing a particular behavior over and over has neurological pathways or grooves in her brain, causing the repetitive pattern. These grooves need diverted, rerouted. She strengthens her prefrontal cortex, the reasoning portion of her brain, by resisting temptation and learning new behaviors. If, when tempted, she chooses a wholesome response to the urge, a newer, healthier pathway forms. This may mean turning away when seeing a sex scene on Netflix, going home on the weekend rather than staying at the dorm, or blocking someone on a social media app.

But why would anyone choose to resist temptation? Why go through the exercise of discerning triggers? What is the underlying motive persuading us to say "no" to an unhealthy behavior or relationship and "yes" to activities that rewire the brain? Why pursue healing after a betrayal? Our relationship with Christ. God helps us by renewing our minds when we surrender to him.

Therefore, I urge you, brothers and sisters, in view of God's mercy, to offer your bodies as a living sacrifice, holy and pleasing to God—this is your true and proper worship. Do not conform to the pattern of this world, but be transformed by the renewing of your mind. Then you will be able to test and approve what God's will is— his good, pleasing and perfect will. (Rom. 12:1–2)

Since you have heard about Jesus and have learned the truth that comes from him, throw off your old sinful nature and your former way of life, which is corrupted by lust and deception. Instead, let the Spirit renew your thoughts and attitudes. Put on your new nature, created to be like God—truly righteous and holy. (Eph. 4:21–24 NLT)

And now, dear brothers and sisters, one final thing. Fix your thoughts on what is true, and honorable, and right, and pure, and lovely, and admirable. Think about things that are excellent and worthy of praise. Keep putting into practice all you learned and received from me— everything you heard from me and saw me doing. Then the God of peace will be with you. (Phil. 4:8–9 NLT)

God's Word and his desire for us to live an abundant life full of his peace is the intrinsic motive inspiring us to get back up when we fall, prompting us to take another step when the mountain seems insurmountable, impelling us to keep going when we want to give up.

> God's Word and his desire for us to live an abundant
> life full of his peace is the intrinsic motive inspiring
> us to get back up when we fall, prompting us to take
> another step when the mountain seems insurmountable,
> impelling us to keep going when we want to give up.

We pursue healing to love others with Christ's love, the love described in 1 Corinthians 13. Healing comes from receiving Christ's love, understanding who we are in Christ, and persevering through the recovery process. Being steeped in his Word, praying fervently, and accepting our identity in Christ heals our injuries and meets our longings. When those triggers materialize, because they will, we can turn from them by adjusting our behavior and filling our minds with truth. When practiced over and over, we are triggered and tempted less and less.

Scars

My son proudly stood on the podium under the award tent at the state meet. The official hung the medal over his head. He hadn't won first place, but he achieved his goal: to compete in the javelin competition at the high school state meet. He endured the hard work, the surgery and crutches, the physical therapy and long workouts. He progressed from using crutches to walking to running. And he won a medal. But he still had scars, visible and invisible. He no longer dreamt of excruciating pain, but he still trembled when he saw an image of someone jumping on a trampoline. He no longer limped, but the scars from his surgery were still noticeable. They will fade with time but will always be with him.

As we heal physically, spiritually, and emotionally, as our wounds mend, we may have scars or tender spots requiring periodic attention. Our scars remind us of our trauma and season of hurt and recovery. But my hope is that the restoration process makes us stronger. As the fourteen-inch rod in my son's leg reinforces it and keeps it from breaking again, God's love, grace, and mercy support us and fortify us. And we are better people for having suffered, endured, and overcome.

8

Reconciliation and Maintaining Healthy Relationships

All this is from God, who reconciled us to himself through
Christ and gave us the ministry of reconciliation. (2 Cor. 5:18)

Lord, help me. I knelt next to my bed, head between my hands. *My son is not who I thought he was. He lives part of his life in a secret world. He has lied to me and purposefully deceived me. I don't know how to look at him or interact with him. Even though I love him fiercely, it hurts to be around him. He needs me, but I'm at a loss on how to help him. I don't trust him, and I don't know if our relationship is fixable. It feels hopeless.*

For months after my son confessed his pornography use, I felt like I was standing on shaky ground. My emotions would sponta- neously escalate for no reason, prompting me to run to my room, kneel at my bed, and cry out to God for strength to finish the day. I wondered if I would recuperate or if our relationship would ever be normal again.

Sexually deviant conduct certainly causes problems in the lives of individuals participating in the behavior. But, as we've discussed throughout the book, it also wreaks havoc on current and future relationships. These may include parent/child relationships, friendships, partners, or marriages. As individuals manage their own issues and trauma by tending to their wounds, they can work on restoring, reconciling, and maintaining healthy relationships.

Let me say up front that sometimes a relationship should be severed. While this chapter focuses on mending relationships, I'm not saying all can be or should be repaired. However, most will pull through if both parties are willing to work on issues together. One unique aspect of a parent/child relationship is its permanency, especially while the child lives at home. Even though a partnership, a friendship, or even a marriage can end, parents typically cannot and should not walk away from a child.

Some preteens, teens, and young adults aren't ready to turn from harmful behaviors. They are unrepentant or uninterested in healthy choices. If you find yourself parenting a child unwilling to reject their unhealthy behaviors, attempt to maintain a loving relationship with them while taking care of yourself. Depending on your child's age and level of maturity, talking with a professional may help. In extreme cases, you may consider a long-term rehabilitation facility or finding a temporary home for your child.

I will assume, for the rest of the book, that all parties involved want personal healing and restored relationships. If you or your child aren't quite ready for reconciliation, don't lose hope. Keep praying. Keep loving. Your story isn't over yet.

Reconciliation

This is the place where everything we've learned comes together. We now understand why relationships are deteriorating and individuals look to outside sources for fulfillment. We've explored how healthy relationships include Christlike love, selflessness, mutuality, and communication. And we've learned that individual healing starts with understanding who we are in Christ. It's time to put all this information into practice.

Restoration of broken relationships includes reconciliation. In Section Two, while exploring habits of healthy relationships, we used 1 Corinthians 13 as the focal point and model of Christlike love. Paul told the Corinthians that love "keeps no record of wrongs" (1 Cor. 13:5). In other words, agape love doesn't hold past behaviors or sins against another person. We don't store up the offenses in our minds or keep a checklist, only to blast our offender with all their wrongdoing whenever we see fit.

God desires for the body of Christ to live in unity, in harmony. A sensible practice of Christian living is resolving conflict in human relations. In 2 Corinthians 5:18, we read that God "gave us the ministry of reconciliation." We can conclude, as many have before us, that a basic facet of restored relationships is reconciliation through extending and seeking forgiveness.

When we forgive, we offer grace, just as God extends grace to us. As a result, we are free from bitterness, anger, hatred, and resentment. Forgiving also has physical health benefits. It can relieve stress, lower blood pressure, and reduce the risk of a heart attack.[1]

Forgiving is not the same as believing the treatment we received is justified. Rather, it's recognizing that Jesus died for the wrongful actions others committed against us and choosing not to hold on to bitterness (keeping no record of wrongs).

Our children learn to extend and seek forgiveness when they observe us modeling the behavior. Note: forgiving a child is separate from parenting a child. But the act of forgiving and the act of hands-on parenting work together. Forgiving frees us to parent without anger and resentment clouding our judgment. In this respect, it's imperative to forgive both for our personal healing and for mending the relationship.

> Forgiving frees us to parent without anger and resentment clouding our judgment.

We may not *feel* like forgiving. We may think the offender should ask for forgiveness or be remorseful first. But we extend forgiveness to our precious ones, even if they don't deserve it or haven't asked for it, for our own sake. This is especially helpful to remember when we need to forgive our teens. We are the adults. We are the parents. We are the authority figures. It's our move. When we interact with our children from love and compassion, not anger and pain, we have more influence over them and we experience more peace.

Years ago, I learned how to forgive while volunteering at Victorious Christian Living International, a discipleship ministry. The following is an adapted version of that teaching:[2]

1. Write what the person did, the offense, and how you felt because of it. For example, as a parent, your list may include: my child lied to me, my child hid an addiction, etc. A teen's list may include: my parent didn't listen to me, my parent screamed at me, my parent doesn't understand what I'm going through, etc. Feelings may include

anger, fear, sorrow, hurt, betrayal, guilt, depression, anxiety, etc.

2. Write the ramifications and/or ripple effects from the incident. These might include a change in routine, loss of independence, financial changes, a modified social life, suicidal thoughts, or altered relationships. Be specific.

3. Itemize your wrongful reactions—for example: screaming, slamming the door, ignoring, parenting from fear, giving the silent treatment, etc.

4. Read through each item on the three lists, and come into agreement with God that Jesus died on the cross for each offense. Forgiving isn't forgetting what happened or saying the offense wasn't real. Instead, it's admitting that Jesus paid the price for each sin, including the ones you committed. "Bear with each other and forgive one another if any of you has a grievance against someone. Forgive as the Lord forgave you" (Col. 3:13).

5. Consider your wrongful reactions. Confess your wrongdoing to God, and ask him if you should seek forgiveness from anyone you've sinned against. "If we confess our sins, he is faithful and just and will forgive us our sins and purify us from all unrighteousness" (1 John 1:9).

6. Pinpoint unrealistic standards, areas in which you expect more of the offender than they can accomplish. For example: my child will perform a specific way, my child will think the way I think, my child can easily quit this nasty habit, etc. A teen might expect a parent to fully understand their day-to-day pressures and circumstances. Dropping expectations saves us from future anger or grief.

While I recommend these forgiveness steps, forgiving is a heart issue. The mere act of walking through this exercise and reciting the words doesn't deliver us from hurts. Releasing the pain and the person inflicting the injury into God's hands is what frees us.

Forgiving is not a onetime event. People repeatedly offend us, so we repeatedly forgive. The good news is, when we release expectations of others, the last step, we aren't agitated as easily. Additionally, when we drop expectations that *we* will behave in a certain way or respond better, we don't feel guilty as often.

After extending forgiveness, seek forgiveness for wrongful actions. As the Holy Spirit leads, approach the one you've wronged, and ask for forgiveness. Admission of wrongful behavior is not a sign of weakness, but a sign of strength. As humans, we all fall short of perfection. Courageously and humbly seeking forgiveness breaks down walls in a relationship and fosters intimacy through vulnerability and honesty.

Modeling Forgiveness

I asked my son if I could speak with him in private. During our last interaction, I had raised my voice and stomped out of the room without listening. "I was wrong to react out of anger during our last conversation. Will you forgive me?"

"Of course, Mom."

Those sweet words washed over me like balm on a wound. I hugged him. "Thank you."

When I sought his forgiveness, I didn't make excuses for my reaction. Nor did I overlook his behavior—it was not acceptable. I didn't change the boundaries we had established. However, my desire for restoration, to walk through the problem together, on the same side, compelled me to repent for my portion of the broken relationship.

When my children were young, I taught them how to forgive and seek forgiveness. I sought their forgiveness when I recognized I wronged them. I hoped my response—asking for forgiveness—would speak louder than the original offense. The long-term goal was for them to carry this practice into adulthood—forgiving and seeking forgiveness of their spouses, coworkers, siblings, church family, and friends.

Forgiving is a step toward rebuilding credibility.

Trust

Trust is broken when a relationship is breached through sexual sins, lies, and deception. As parents, we can help our children rebuild trust inside and outside the home, as well as prepare them for future hurdles. Integrity may be more difficult to establish in new relationships when these behaviors are part of someone's past. That's normal and should be expected.

Ultimately, believing someone else requires a leap of faith. When I married for the second time, I dealt with trust issues. Because my first marriage had ended, I worried about my second husband dying or otherwise leaving me. These doubts affected the marriage. One day, God showed me he was bigger than the relationship. He told me to lean on him. When I acted in faith, assuming my husband and I would have a long-lasting relationship, I was trusting God, the One who could and would sustain me. I have little control over my husband's actions. I can't stop him from dying in an accident, contracting a terminal illness, or having an affair and leaving me. However, I have faith in God, and I have faith in his promptings, which tell me to believe in my husband.

Now, based on our history and experience together, I trust Don because I know his intentions are pure and his actions prove it.

How do we believe in our children again when they've violated our trust? How do they become trustworthy to a potential spouse? Dependability is not rebuilt overnight. Be patient. Full restoration comes in stages. As your children heal internally, help them establish boundaries, reconnect with those they've hurt, put accountability measures in place, and set long-term goals.

> As your children heal internally, help them establish boundaries, reconnect with those they've hurt, put accountability measures in place, and set long-term goals.

Remind your children to be patient with and respect those they've hurt. They crossed a line and need to win trust back. They should be willing to prove that their word is reliable. These traits require humbleness, persistence, and strength. Redirect them to God and his Word. While regaining trust, they can lean on the One who identifies them as loved, adopted, forgiven, and redeemed.

Boundaries

In Chapter Five, we discussed the definition and importance of boundaries. We also looked at setting and communicating boundaries. Individuals hurt by hookup culture, steeped in pornography use, or lost in an online world of social media, gaming, or other screen addictions need boundaries specific to their tendency, as well as boundaries within relationships. Help your children understand the purpose of these extra safeguards.

As the hurt one, talk openly about your emotions. Explain why certain rules are necessary for *your* comfort. For example, your teen may choose not to take devices into the bedroom or bathroom for their personal protection and healing. But your comfort zone may be narrower. Perhaps you'd rather your child use devices only in your presence, at least temporarily. This request may appear extreme, but if your teen wants to prove their dependability, they may agree to this standard.

Of course, as a parent, you have every right to impose rules without asking permission, but we want to usher our teens into adulthood by helping them learn to willingly yield to others' needs. We want them to understand that actions have consequences and to desire to put the welfare of others in front of their own. "Do nothing out of selfish ambition or vain conceit. Rather, in humility value others above yourselves, not looking to your own interests but each of you to the interests of the others" (Phil. 2:3–4).

When my son broke my trust, he agreed to several terms as part of his rehabilitation program and to regain our confidence. One understanding was that I would periodically search his devices without warning. About once a week, for several months, when he was on his computer or phone, I asked what he was doing. He answered me, but then, for my peace of mind, I requested the computer or phone, looked at his open tabs or apps, and searched his history. He could have been angry because I didn't believe him. Instead, he obliged with a respectful attitude because he knew I needed reassurance, through verifying his answers, that he was telling the truth.

As my son healed and rebuilt trust within our relationship, we loosened the boundaries. Years into his recovery, he disclosed his issues and limitations to his girlfriend. He was prepared to hear how his past behaviors affected their relationship and establish any safeguards she requested.

Boundaries help create new patterns, which lead to healthier habits. Sometimes, within a relationship, behaviors feed off each other. For example, if I believe my husband is ignoring me, I instinctually bark at him using loud, abrupt tones. He, in turn, defends himself using a condescending tone. And round and round it goes. Even if I learn, in the middle of our spat, he *wasn't* ignoring me, it's too late to stop the descending spiral. We're caught in this pattern we began years ago. Our brains have slid down those deep grooves we created throughout our marriage.

The objective is to stop the pattern by recognizing the trigger (I'm being ignored), know the reason the trigger is a trigger (I've bought into the lie that I'm not worth paying attention to), and create a new method of responding to the trigger (quoting Scripture related to who I am in Christ and taking a deep breath before continuing the conversation). If I clue my husband in to my thought process, how I feel when I believe he's ignoring me, he can also work on changing his reactions.

The key is for both parties to communicate emotions, triggers, harmful responses, and requests. For example, if someone believes she's a failure, a loser, or ugly, and if she self-medicates through harmful behavior, she can disclose this information to the other. Then, together, they can devise a new strategy to counteract the negative self-talk and destructive behaviors.

The relationship deteriorates if one person suffers in silence. Be humble and honoring, but speak openly and honestly about how your inner thoughts affect your own behaviors or how the other person's actions affect you. Without blaming, suggest an alternate method for dealing with negative emotions or triggers. This is a back-and-forth discussion. Both contribute thoughts and suggestions.

It's an intricate balance. We want to forgive when another person mistreats us, and we want to let go of our expectations. At the same time, we seek forgiveness for our wrongdoings, do our best to correct our sinful behavior, and communicate how we feel when someone behaves a particular way. If both people are respectful and loving and have the other's best interest in mind, these conversations are freeing and lead to a more intimate connection.

> If both people are respectful and loving and have the other's best interest in mind, these conversations are freeing and lead to a more intimate connection.

Reconnect

Each of us creates a space for ourselves. We visit the same spots, interact with the same people, browse the same social media apps, etc. These actions produce a space in which we feel comfortable. We tend to reinforce thought patterns by subconsciously hanging out with people who think the way we think and believe the way we believe. Internet algorithms fortify those patterns. If we search for a certain candidate's views on a topic or research a medical ailment, our feed and sponsored advertisements lean in that direction. (If you don't believe me, search for a cruise to the Caribbean and see how the ads change in your email feed, etc.)

We're influenced by what we see and hear, especially if the messages are reinforced through social interactions and the media. For example, when I first saw someone wearing loose-fitting ripped jeans, I didn't like the style. Now I have a pair and think they're my cutest jeans.

Unfortunately, by narrowing our sphere of influence, the space we roam about in, we can miss the big picture and be close-minded to other perspectives.

How we view people in general affects how we respond to individuals. And that, in turn, can make or break a relationship. It can define a relationship as toxic or healthy. When our teens' brains are trained to believe people are violent or full of hatred because of the messages in hookup culture, pornography, and gaming, help them reframe their thinking to correct those beliefs.

During the restoration process, the hurting parties may need to relearn how to connect with others, to reconnect in a healthier manner. If teens believe parents are cruel because all adults are mean, we can help them see us as loving. If we view our teens as disgusting because of their behaviors, we can reframe our thinking by studying Scripture, reminding ourselves they're created in the image of God, and remembering they're victims of society.

If our teens have a difficult time bonding in real life because their brains are conditioned to bond with screens, nurture the in-person relationship. This is a process. It takes time and patience to rewire the brain and find a new system of connecting. Discuss activities to cultivate the bonding process. Play board games, go for walks or bike rides, sit at the dining room table together while working. Find a common interest, like playing the piano or fishing. Search for conversation starters online to foster discussions during supper. Put your phone down and look them in the eye.

Connecting in a way you both feel heard and valued takes trial and error. Both parties should be willing to disclose emotions and thoughts not typically said. This requires courage and vulnerability.

Accountability

Six months after my son's second confession, I stuck my head in his bedroom. "Do you have time for a walk with me?"

"Sure."

He put his shoes on, and we left the house.

"How's your day going?" I asked as we stepped onto the sidewalk.

"Fine. I finished my homework and was looking through my baseball cards."

"Great. Did you sleep through the night?"

"Mostly. I only woke up once, but I stayed in bed and went back to sleep fairly quickly."

"Excellent. That's progress." I looked at him and smiled. "Any struggles in the past day?"

"I was tempted earlier by something I saw, but I left the room and started working a math problem in my head. I'm okay now."

I didn't see or hear any signs of deception. I was working through my betrayal issues, and his candor was a positive step toward restoring our relationship. "Thanks for being honest. I'm proud of you. Let me know how I can help you."

"Thanks, Mom."

We switched the subject to something more lighthearted as we finished our walk.

We can't do life alone. Isolation leads to sadness and depression. Keeping secrets accelerates this process. To succeed, to flourish, to maintain healthy relationships, expose what has been in the darkness to light. Find a friend, a confidante, or trusted adult and talk about your innermost thoughts and emotions.

> To succeed, to flourish, to maintain healthy relationships, expose what has been in the darkness to light.

Until my son was sixteen and confessed he was still watching pornography, we kept his secret among him, his dad, and me. I told one friend, but none of his siblings or anyone else knew. When he came to us the second time, I probed further into his issue, asking questions about his first exposure to pornography and its continued presence in his life. He hesitated and gave me halfhearted answers. He desired freedom but also wanted to protect others. I understood his tentativeness but knew he couldn't heal without full disclosure.

I told him, "We need to live in the light. That means we expose the truth. If we keep secrets in the dark, they gain power. When we bring them into the light, they lose power." My words prompted him to reveal the stronghold pornography had in his life. He disclosed the information surrounding his initial experience and continued use. That was the beginning of his healing process.

Rewiring our brains, changing our habits, and breaking our addictions requires an admission of wrongful behaviors, turning from those deeds, and replacing them with new, healthier choices. These new actions only stick if they are undergirded with proper thoughts about who we are in Christ. This process is almost impossible without accountability.

Healthy relationships include accountability. In a marriage, each person is accountable to the other. In parent/child relationships, the weight is shifted. The child is accountable to the parent, but the parent is responsible for putting accountability factors in place and consistently checking on the progress of both the child's recovery and the restoration of the relationship.

Elements of accountability after a breach of trust vary based on the initial issue and the strength of the relationship. A college student escaping hookup culture may send a text to a friend every night at 9:30 p.m. stating her whereabouts. Someone struggling with online gaming may check in with a friend each morning to report the time she went to bed the night before and how many hours she slept. A teen struggling with pornography may talk with a trusted adult each evening, disclosing any temptations she encountered.

Whatever the problem, ongoing conversations are necessary to rebuild relationships. As a parent, initiate discussions about social media, sexuality, online grooming, bullying, pornography, and other hot topics. Ask about the presenting issue. Become the expert and their go-to source. Ask open-ended questions, and actively listen to show you are committed to their life and the relationship. Be vulnerable by talking about your weaknesses and past feelings. Apply those communication skills we talked about in Chapter Six.

Along with deep discussions, schedule daily check-in conversations. Set aside five to ten minutes each day for a private talk specifically about the tempting behavior. Ask about their day. Inquire about triggers, emotions, and temptations. Ask about successes and failures. Listen without judgment. Congratulate victories, and be supportive when there are setbacks. These actions are important steps toward rebuilding trust. Even when your child stumbles, if they're truthful, walls are broken down and mending takes place.

Goals

As part of the accountability element and rebuilding trust, set short-term and long-term goals, as individuals and within relationships. These goals may include:

- ▸ Daily check-in conversations over a particular period of time
- ▸ Reading through Scripture together daily
- ▸ Attending a support group or a program
- ▸ Staying clean for "X" number of days, weeks, or months
- ▸ Participating in a fun joint activity monthly
- ▸ Staying within screen time limits
- ▸ Using relaxation methods
- ▸ Adding an exercise routine
- ▸ Revamping a diet
- ▸ Creating a plan to counteract triggers

Use these suggestions as a starting point. Add more to personalize your situation.

In addition to establishing goals related to healing, set goals for the future. What accomplishments do you and your children want to achieve, individually and within the relationship, in the next month? Six months? Year? Five years?

Goals remind us we have a purpose. They're a reason to get out of bed every morning and engage in life. When we set realistic short-term goals and achieve them, our spirits are boosted and we're motivated to accomplish more.

> Goals remind us we have a purpose.

Our goals should be rooted in our identity in Christ. When they grow from our God-given abilities, skills, and personalities, we're apt to be excited about them, put energy into them, and reach them.

Study God's Word and pray about next steps. Encourage and support your children as they set goals. Believe in them. They are created in God's image, and he has implanted desires, dreams, and aspirations into their innermost being. Dive deep into their lives and inspire them to live big—to reach for the yearnings God ingrained in them.

Looking Forward

My husband, daughter, son, and I sat around the dinner table. My twenty-year-old son was home from college on Christmas break and was entertaining us with humorous anecdotes of his roommates.

Between stories, I asked, "What's next? What are your upcoming plans?"

"My class load for my last semester is pretty light. I've applied for master's programs at two universities. I'm hoping to attend the one near my girlfriend . . . and we've looked at rings."

"That's fantastic!" My heart leapt. "I'm so proud of you and excited about your future. You are adulting well. You've confronted your issues, overcome several obstacles, and achieved many of your goals. I love your girlfriend and look forward to celebrating your engagement."

I was overwhelmed with emotions—pride, delight, contentment, joy, *and* happiness. Yes, happiness. Not the *as long as* type of happiness, but the kind that overflows from peace and joy.

My son and I worked through our issues. He proved his credibility to me. He isn't perfect. Neither am I. But our relationship is healthy, and I'm proud of the man he has become. He has a solid relationship with Christ and has learned to be still and face his problems, not run from them. He has confessed his past issues to his girlfriend and helped her understand that part of his life. Since that dinner table conversation, he completed his bachelor's degree despite quarantines and injuries, asked that girlfriend to marry him, and is looking forward to the next stage of life.

The Greatest Is Love

"Love never fails. . . . And now these three remain: faith, hope and love. But the greatest of these is love" (1 Cor. 13:8, 13).

As we come to the end of our time together, let's look at this last line of the "love chapter." We've explored Christlike love and many of its facets. We've probed how our identity in Christ affects our beliefs, behaviors, and interactions. Now let's see how these three—faith, hope, and love—work together. Paul says when we have faith without love, it's nothing. We can possess material items, physical abilities, and even gifts from God, but they are worthless without love. It's love that never fails, but faith and hope allow God's love to pour from us to others. When we have faith and exercise hope, God's love prevails. And when we have faith covered in love, we have hope.

That's what God wants to leave you with—hope—for you and your children.

The next generation is resilient. They are enlightened, passionate, and want to make a difference. Gen Zers and millennials are self-aware, loving, smart, fun, and full of life. They are sensitive and care about the environment, their friends, and the future.

These individuals want to learn and interact with the community and those in their sphere of influence. They want to impact the world. The next generation feels intensely, takes life seriously, and knows how to have fun. They are amazing individuals.

Let's come alongside them and cheer for them. Let's cultivate the best parts of them by loving them with Christlike love. Let's remind them that they are unique, precious, and made in the image of God.

When we nurture, promote, and support the next generation, they will be inspired. They will influence their peers and the generation behind them to have healthy relationships. They will leave their impression on the world.

And so will you.

Acknowledgments

Wow! What a ride. When I began encouraging other parents who were trying to navigate this crazy online world, I didn't picture myself publishing a book. When God said to write one, I felt a little nauseous. And underqualified. But I began, starting with one paragraph and then another. Eventually, it all came together. And I'm blessed because of it. I hope you are too.

Of course, no one writes a book alone, so allow me a moment to acknowledge those who encouraged, supported, pushed, prayed, and, frankly, put up with me throughout the process.

To Don, my husband, best friend, and biggest cheerleader: thanks for teaching me Christlike love and believing in me when I didn't believe in myself, picking me up when I felt down, and standing by me in good times and bad. You're my rock in the flesh.

To Kenneth, my son and my hero: thanks for teaching me the meaning of perseverance, self-discipline, and laughter. You have forever changed me for the better.

To JT, my son: thanks for teaching me my heart wouldn't break when more love than I knew existed poured out of it onto you, my firstborn. And thanks for teaching me how to let go.

To Melinda, my favorite daughter: thanks for teaching me how to fight for my children, be a cheerful giver, and keep emotions in check. I'm still working on that last one. I hope our friendship endures.

To Kevin, my stepson: thanks for teaching me how to love selflessly.

To my prayer team—Marsha Young, Dena Yohe, Christy Bass Adams, Ava Pennington, David Rawls, Jen Cason, Janice Summers, Melinda Winters, and Don Winters: thanks for having my back.

To my Hope Community Church family, especially my connection group and the ladies' group: thanks for listening to me ramble, coaxing me forward, and offering me a place to be me.

To the E3 Family Solutions team, my bosses and coworkers: thanks for believing in me, training me, and offering opportunities to talk about the subjects close to my heart.

To Ava Pennington and my two Word Weavers critique groups: thanks for reading, tweaking, and improving my writing.

To Marilyn Evans, Vauna Davis, and The Safeguard Alliance: thanks for drawing me into your fold and treating me like an equal.

To Blythe Daniel, my agent: thanks for seeing potential in my writing and taking a chance on me. I'm humbled and forever grateful.

To Leafwood Publishers: thanks for believing in this message. I pray parents are blessed because of your generosity.

To you, the reader: thanks for spending your hard-earned money on this book. I pray it encourages and inspires you.

And to Jesus, my true rock: thanks for placing the passion in my heart and the words in my head. My hope comes from you.

Notes

CHAPTER ONE

[1] "A Quote by Elisabeth Elliot," Goodreads, accessed December 16, 2022, https://www.goodreads.com/quotes/27241-the-world-looks-for-happiness-through-self-assertion-the-christian-knows.

[2] Andrea Davis, "Glow Kids: Research That Will Motivate You to Create a Plan," Better Screen Time, September 21, 2018, https://www.betterscreentime.com/glow-kids-one-of-my-top-book-recommendations/.

[3] Justin R. Garcia, Chris Reiber, Sean G. Massey, and Ann M. Merriwether, "Sexual Hookup Culture: A Review," *Review of General Psychology* 16, no. 2 (June 1, 2012): 161–76, https://pubmed.ncbi.nlm.nih.gov/23559846/.

[4] Donna Freitas, "A Good Samaritan Response to Hookup Culture," the Institute for Faith and Learning at Baylor University, 2016, https://www.baylor.edu/content/services/document.php/277019.pdf, 39–41.

[5] Freitas, "Good Samaritan Response," 41.

[6] *New Girl*, season 1, episode 1, "Pilot," directed by Jake Kasdan, aired September 20, 2011, on FOX.

[7] *New Girl*, season 1, episode 3, "Wedding," directed by Jason Winer, aired October 4, 2011, on FOX.

[8] "*New Girl* (2011–2018): Awards," IMDb, accessed September 24, 2021, https://m.imdb.com/title/tt1826940/awards/?ref_=tt_awd; Allison Mann, "Eight Reasons Why *New Girl* Has Stayed Popular for So Long," TheThings, March 8, 2022, https://www.thethings.com/why-new-girl-stayed-popular-so-long/.

[9] Justin R. Garcia et al., "Sexual Hook-up Culture," *Monitor on Psychology* 44, no. 2 (February 2013): 60, https://www.apa.org/monitor/2013/02/ce-corner.

[10] Lisa Wade, *American Hookup: The New Culture of Sex on Campus* (New York: W. W. Norton & Company, 2018), 58–59.

[11] "The Pill and the Sexual Revolution," PBS, accessed October 19, 2021, https://www.pbs.org/wgbh/americanexperience/features/pill-and-sexual-revolution/.

[12] Wade, *American Hookup*, 75.

[13] Camille Mori, Jessica E. Cooke, Jeff R. Temple, Anh Ly, Yu Lu, Nina Anderson, Christina Rash, and Sheri Madigan, "The Prevalence of Sexting Behaviors among Emerging Adults: A Meta-Analysis," *Archives of Sexual Behavior* 49, no. 4 (May 2020): 1103–19, https://pubmed.ncbi.nlm.nih.gov/32072397/.

[14] "What Is Child Sexual Abuse Material (CSAM)," RAINN, August 25, 2022, https://www.rainn.org/news/what-child-sexual-abuse-material-csam.

CHAPTER TWO

[1]"Personality Animal Profiles," The Center for Relationship Education, accessed December 17, 2022, https://www.myrelationshipcenter.org/resources/personality-animal-profiles.

[2]Wade, *American Hookup*, 145–46.

[3]Casey Gwinn, "What Are the Risks of Choking a Partner during Sex?," Fight the New Drug, accessed December 18, 2022, https://fightthenewdrug.org/the-concerning-trend-of-porn-romanticizing-strangulation/; Alexandra Sifferlin, "Here's What Sexist Video Games Do to Boys' Brains," *Time*, April 13, 2016, https://time.com/4290455/heres-what-sexist-video-games-do-to-boys-brains/; "Protecting Children Online," UNICEF, February 8, 2021, https://www.unicef.org/protection/violence-against-children-online.

[4]Wade, *American Hookup*, 15 and 223.

CHAPTER THREE

[1]Brittany Shammas, "Judge Awards $13 Million to Women Who Say They Were Tricked into Pornography," *The Washington Post*, January 4, 2020, https://www.washingtonpost.com/business/2020/01/03/judge-awards-million-women-who-say-they-were-tricked-into-pornography/.

[2]Katie Burton, "Pornography and Sex Trafficking—a Vicious Cycle," Nebraska Family Alliance, January 30, 2017, https://nebraskafamilyalliance.org/pornography-and-sex-trafficking-a-vicious-cycle/.

CHAPTER FOUR

[1]Lisa Eldred, "Purity Culture and Its Unfortunate Intersection with Porn," Covenant Eyes, November 3, 2021, https://www.covenanteyes.com/2021/09/28/purity-culture-and-porn/.

[2]Eldred, "Purity Culture."

CHAPTER FIVE

[1]Robert Jensen, "Porn Increasingly Normalizes Sexual Violence and Racism, So Why Is It Still So Popular?," Fight the New Drug, accessed December 20, 2022, https://fightthenewdrug.org/porn-normalizes-sexual-violence-and-racism-so-why-is-it-still-popular/.

[2]Sifferlin, "Here's What Sexist Video Games Do to Boys' Brains."

[3]Gary Chapman, *The 5 Love Languages: The Secret to Love that Lasts* (Northfield, VT: Northfield Publishing, 2015).

CHAPTER EIGHT

[1]"Forgiveness: Your Health Depends on It," Johns Hopkins Medicine, November 1, 2021, https://www.hopkinsmedicine.org/health/wellness-and-prevention/forgiveness-your-health-depends-on-it.

[2]Victorious Christian Living International, *Victorious Christian Living Conference: Training in Biblical Discipleship* (Kearney, NE: Morris Publishing, 1999).